the Knit Hat book

the **Knit Hat** book

25 Hats
from Basic Shapes

NICKY EPSTEIN

Photographs by Marcus Tullis

Taunton
BOOKS & VIDEOS
for fellow enthusiasts

Printed in the United States of America
10 9 8 7 6 5 4 3 2 1

A THREADS Book
THREADS® is a trademark of The Taunton Press, Inc.,
registered in the U.S. Patent and Trademark Office.

The Taunton Press, Inc., 63 South Main Street, PO Box 5506,
Newtown, CT 06470-5506
e-mail: tp@taunton.com

Library of Congress Cataloging-in-Publication Data

Epstein, Nicky.
    The knit hat book : 25 hats from basic shapes / Nicky Epstein.
        p.   cm.
        ISBN 1-56158-199-2
    1. Knitting–Patterns. 2. Hats. I. Title
    TT825.E64   1997   97-16543
    746.43'20432–dc21   CIP

To Anna and Carmella,
who made my life so rich

Acknowledgments

*A special thank you to Howard,
my loving critic and adviser, and to
my hat knitters, Eileen Curry,
Shelley Charney, and Jackie Smyth.*

Contents

Introduction

There's an old saying, "If a woman feels depressed, the best antidote is to go out and buy a new hat." I've discovered that a far better solution (and not only for depression) is to knit your own hat! It is immensely satisfying to create your own hat for yourself or a loved one. Whether for warmth, for fashion, or to make a personal statement, knitting a hat is an easy, quick, inexpensive, and creatively rewarding experience for the knitter, and it makes a unique accessory for the wearer. I've created many hat designs for publications, but I also love to knit hats both for myself and for my family and friends. I've written this book to share with my fellow knitters the enormous gratification that I get when I knit a hat.

In this book, I've included easy-to-follow instructions for many traditional hat styles, as well as laid the groundwork for you to create your own designs. You'll find basic hat shape instructions, texture stitches, intarsia charts, embroidery, and appliqué patterns and techniques. You'll also learn how to make pom-poms, tassels, and ties. Your horizons are as broad as your imagination.

Yarn colors are always coming and going. In trying to keep up with color trends, yarn companies introduce new colors and discontinue old ones every season. I've listed the colors that were used to make the hats in the photos, but they may not all be available when you decide to start knitting. Use your own taste and judgment in making substitutions—I'm sure you'll get wonderful results. Hats are perfect to use up odd balls of yarn and to experiment with colors, so have fun! You will come up with a hat that is all yours.

The variations to hat designing are endless, and you'll soon discover your own personal creative preferences. My goal in designing hats professionally has always been to make the hat design unique. That is what you will eventually be able to do as I show you how to use stitches, bobbles, cord, textures, flowers, leaves, and other techniques to create a knitted hat that is distinctive. You'll be proud to wear your creations and proud to give them as gifts.

I've enjoyed teaching many knitting classes throughout my career, and the enthusiasm and creativity of students in my hat classes has been so satisfying that it became my inspiration for this book.

I welcome you to the world of knitted hats. This is one experience where you can let the beautiful results go to your head!

Happy hat knitting!

Basics

GAUGE

Even on a project as small as a hat and whether you use the suggested yarn or an alternate yarn, it is essential that you check the gauge. Using the needles and stitch recommended in the pattern, knit a sample that is at least 4½ in. wide and 4½ in. long. Without stretching this swatch, count exactly how many stitches there are in the 4-in. width and exactly how many rows in the 4-in. length. Fractions should be counted. This is your gauge. If you have more stitches than recommended, try again using larger needles. If you have fewer stitches than recommended, try using smaller needles.

If the completed hat is too big or too small, don't panic! Unlike an ill-fitting sweater that can be difficult to adjust, hat size is fairly easy to adjust. If your hat is too small, with no seam, try blocking it out. If it has a seam, leave the seam open 1 in. to 1½ in. at the bottom and add a tassel, bow, or button. If the hat is too big and has no seam, adjust the size by making a tuck, pleat, or gather. Adding elastic is another option. Even if your hat fits properly, elastic around the base will ensure that your hat keeps its shape.

YARN SUBSTITUTION

To duplicate the hats in the book you can use the suggested yarn, or you can use yarns you may have left over from other projects. Most hats only take a few skeins of yarn, so you can even splurge with yarns like angora, cashmere, or some expensive blends. It's always pleasant to see one of my designs being worn, but it's even more gratifying to see a knitter's personal variations on a design that I originally inspired. Never hesitate to give the hat your own creative touches.

BLOCKING

Always consider the fiber you are using when blocking. Wool fibers do well with steam and wet blocking, but acrylic fibers lose body, which can ruin the hat. It's a good idea to test-block your gauge swatch.

Novelty yarns such as chenille and furs require no blocking. The hats in Chapter 1 require light blocking, which should be done before appliqués are added. The berets in Chapter 2 and the Bow Jest hat in Chapter 3 require blocking to shape them. To block any of these, place it over a 10-in. or 11-in. plate. Steam it, let it dry, and then remove it from the plate. The pillbox hats in Chapter 4 require light steam blocking. To shape any of these hats, place it over a cooking pot that is 7 in. in diameter. The cooking pot should be upside down. Steam the hat lightly using a cloth between the hat and the steam iron. Let the hat dry and then remove it from the pot. The only hats in Chapter 5 that require light steaming are the Fleur-de-Lys and the Double-Take Snowflake.

SEAMING

I recommend the mattress stitch for seaming most hats. This stitch makes an invisible seam and is worked from the right side. You can also use a back stitch, but it is worked with right sides together.

Mattress stitch

With right sides together and the edges of the work side by side, make a join at the lower edge. Insert the needle between the first and second stitch, pick up one horizontal bar, and draw the thread through. *Insert the needle under two horizontal bars on the alternate side and draw the thread through. Repeat from * for the seam.

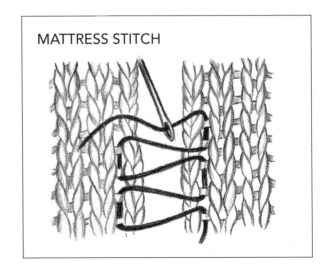

MATTRESS STITCH

Back stitch

With right sides facing, lay the two pieces of work together, matching up row for row as closely as possible. Pin the edges together or baste about two stitches in from the edge. Back stitch the pieces together one stitch in, keeping the stitching parallel to the edge of the work.

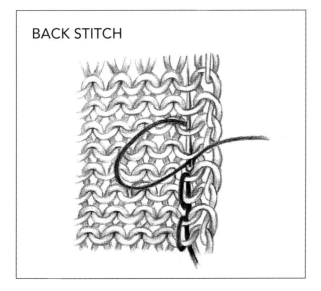

BACK STITCH

DUPLICATE STITCH

Duplicate stitch is an embroidery stitch used on stockinette stitch. It is called duplicate stitch because it duplicates the stitch below it. It is formed by retracing the path of the original stitch and thereby covering it. Connect the yarn at the right-hand side where the embroidered line is desired. From the back, place the needle at the base of the first stitch you want to cover. Pull toward the front. Pass the needle under the two loops of the same stitch, going from right to left. Pull through. Go back into the base of the same stitch from front to back. Place the needle into the base of the next stitch from the back, and repeat for as many stitches as desired. Duplicate stitch is used in the Moon Trees, Hugs 'n Kisses, and Music Box hats.

HEAD SIZES

These are approximate circumferences of an adult head:

- Extra small—20 in.
- Small—21 in.
- Medium—22 in.
- Large—23 in.
- Extra large—24 in.

ABBREVIATIONS

alt	alternate	rh	right hand
approx	approximately	rnd(s)	round(s)
beg	begin(ning)	rs	right side(s)
cc	contrasting color	sl	slip
C4F	slip 2 stitches to cable needle and hold at front of work, knit 2, knit 2 from cable needle	sl st	slip stitch: Pass stitch from left-hand to right-hand needle as if to purl (unless otherwise specified) without working it.
ch	chain stitch		
cn	cable needle	ssk	slip, slip, knit: Slip next 2 stitches knitwise, one at a time to right-hand needle. Insert tip of left-hand needle into fronts of these stitches from left to right and knit them together.
cont	continue(ing)		
dec	decrease(ing)		
g	gram(s)		
garter st	garter stitch: Knit every row. When knitting circularly, knit one round, then purl one round.		
		st st	stockinette stitch: Knit right-side rows, purl wrong-side rows. When knitting circularly, knit every round.
in.	inch(es)		
inc	increase(ing)	st(s)	stitch(es)
k	knit	tbl	through back loop(s)
knitwise	Insert needle into stitch as if to knit.	tog	together
m	meter(s)	work even	Continue to work in established stitch or pattern without increasing or decreasing.
mc	main color		
oz.	ounce(s)		
p	purl	ws	wrong side(s)
patt(s)	pattern(s)	wyib	with yarn in back
psso	pass slipped stitch(es) over	wyif	with yarn in front
purlwise	Insert needle into stitch as if to purl.	yd.	yard(s)
		yo	yarn over needle
rem	remain(ing)	*	repeat from * as many times as indicated
rep	repeat		
rev st st	reverse stockinette stitch: Purl right-side rows, knit wrong-side rows. When knitting circularly, purl every round.	[ ]	repeat directions inside [ ] as many times as indicated

Caps

The hats in this chapter derive their inspiration from nature.
They are designed to be unique yet functional. I started with the
basic cap shape and created a variety of crown-shaping and
edging techniques to give them their own individuality.

Knit appliqués are special stitch formations (or patterns)
that lend themselves beautifully to hat designs. In this chapter,
you'll find instructions for various appliqué patterns to make
trees, acorns, leaves, grapes, and berries. By adding these
appliqués to a basic shape, you can create a variety of caps
without a great deal of effort.

Clockwise from top:
Acorn Autumn with ear flaps and ties,
Beaujolais, Berry Nice

Basic Cap Instructions

If you are using a patterned stitch, be aware of stitch multiples and row repeats when working your gauge, sizing your instructions, or adding selvage stitches. When knitting in the round, selvage stitches are not needed.

The following patterns are for two basic cap shapes. These shapes are the basic pattern for each of the embellished versions of caps in this chapter. Feel free to create your own unique caps using these basic shapes.

SAMPLE 1

Sample 1 is worked in simple stockinette stitch, cast on the number of stitches equal to the head circumference multiplied by stitches per inch as determined by gauge. Work even to desired length from the beginning—usually 6 in. to 8 in. for an adult depending on the lower edging. Decrease over the last 3 rows as follows for crown shaping.

Dec row 1 (rs) K2 tog across.
Dec row 2 P2 tog across.
Dec row 3 K2 tog across.
Cut yarn, leaving long end. With tapestry needle, thread end through rem sts on needle.
Gather up and fasten securely.

SAMPLE 2

Sample 2 demonstrates the relationship between gauge, head size, and the amount of stitches needed for the cap. More evenly distributed decreases form a decorative crown shaping. This example is worked in stockinette stitch over 100 (107, 114) stitches including 2 selvage stitches for seaming. The gauge is 20 stitches and 26 rows to 4 in. for a finished head size of approximately 19½ (21, 22½) in. Work even to desired length from beginning, ending on wrong side approximately 2 in. less than total desired length of hat. Continue with crown shaping as follows:

Small (medium, large)
Row 1 K1, *k2 tog, k5; rep from *, k1—86 (92, 98) sts.
Even rows 2-8 Purl.
Row 3 K1, *k2 tog, k4; rep from *, k1—72 (77, 82) sts.
Row 5 K1, *k2 tog, k3; rep from *, k1—58 (62, 66) sts.
Row 7 K1, *k2 tog, k2; rep from *, k1—44 (47, 50) sts.
Row 9 K1, *k2 tog; rep from *, end k1 (2, 1)—
23 (25, 26) sts.
Row 10 P1 (2, 1) *p2 tog; rep from *, end p2 (1, 1)—
13 (14, 14) sts.
Row 11 K1 (0, 0), *k2 tog; rep from *,—7 sts.
Cut yarn, leaving long end. With tapestry needle, thread end through rem sts on needle.
Gather up and fasten securely.

LOWER EDGES

Rolled edge

To create a rolled edge, work in stockinette stitch from the beginning. Stockinette has a natural tendency to roll back on itself. Depending on the weight and fiber content of the yarn, the amount of "roll" may vary, so take this into consideration when determining the length of work before shaping the crown. If the yarn isn't very elastic, you may want to come down a needle size or two for the roll.

Ribbed edge

Ribbing can add a decorative touch as well as creating a snug edge that hugs the head. Consider patterned or cable ribs as alternatives to classic 1x1 and 2x2 variations. Make a swatch first to see how compatible the rib pattern is with the main stitch pattern. Using a different needle size or altering the number of stitches used in the rib to accommodate pattern multiples may be necessary to achieve the desired results. The depth of the ribbing should be figured into the length worked even before shaping the crown.

DESIGNER TIP

If you've ever started a sweater (front or back) and for some reason abandoned it to a closet or dresser drawer, you can give it new life. Make a hat out of it by working a crown shaping! Some of my most successful hats were born this way. A sweater front or back is usually between 20 in. and 24 in. wide, and the size of an average head is around 22 in., so you've got the makings of a great hat. Sweaters that have a rib knit are particularly good because of their elasticity. With the yarn you have left over from the original purchase, you can make at least three more hats!

Acorn Autumn

Because each hat I make is unique, I haven't provided exact color and placement of the leaves and acorns. Use your own creativity with colors and placement. This hat can be made with or without the ear flaps and ties.

SIZE

Small (medium, large)
Directions are for smallest size, with larger sizes in parentheses. If only one figure appears, it applies to all sizes.

MATERIALS

Yarn

Tahki Donegal Tweed, 3½ oz./100 g skein; each about 183 yd./167 m:

- **A** Brown 860—1 skein
- **B** Gold 802—small amount
- **C** Dark Green 878—small amount
- **D** Olive 846—small amount
- **E** Red 840—small amount

Needles

- Size 7, or size required to obtain correct gauge
- Size 7 double-pointed needles
- Size F crochet hook

Other

- Tapestry needle
- Fiberfill—small amount

GAUGE

18 sts and 24 rows = 4 in. in st st
To save time, take time to check gauge.

NOTES

Stitch counts in the directions include two selvage stitches for seaming.

HAT

With A, cast on 95 (100, 105) sts [93 (98, 103) patt sts + 2 selvage sts].
Work even in st st for 7½ in.; end ws.

Crown shaping

Dec row 1 (rs) K2 (1, 2), *k2 tog; rep from * to last st, k1—49 (51, 54) sts.

Dec row 2 (ws) P2 (2, 1), *p2 tog; rep from * to last st, p1—26 (27, 28) sts.

Dec row 3 (rs) K1 (2, 1), *k2 tog; rep from * to last st, k1—14 (15, 15) sts.

Cut yarn, leaving long end. With tapestry needle, thread end through rem sts on needle.
Gather up and fasten securely.

Ear flaps (make 2)

With A, cast on 21 sts.
Work even in st st for 4 rows.

Next row (rs) K1, ssk, k to last 3 sts, k2 tog, k1—19 sts.

Following row Purl.

Rep last 2 rows until 5 sts rem; end ws.

Next row (rs) K1, sl 2 sts tog knitwise, k1, pass 2 sl sts over, k1—3 sts.

Following row Purl.

Tie

Change to double-pointed needles and work I-cord over rem 3 sts: *K across. Do not turn work. Push the sts back to rh end of needle. Pull to tighten and rep from * until cord measures 14 in. or desired length.
Bind off.
Knot end of each tie.

LEAVES

(make 5 small and 1 large)

Use colors B, C, D, and E, changing colors mid-row as desired.

Small leaves

Cast on 5 sts.

Row 1 (rs) K2, yo, k1, yo, k2—7 sts.

Row 2 Purl.

Row 3 K3, yo, k1, yo, k3—9 sts.

Row 4 Purl.

Row 5 K4, yo, k1, yo, k4—11 sts.

Row 6 Purl.

Row 7 Bind off 3 sts, k1, yo, k1, yo, k5—10 sts.

Row 8 Bind off 3 sts, p6—7 sts.

Row 9 K3, yo, k1, yo, k3—9 sts.

Row 10 Purl.

Row 11 K4, yo, k1, yo, k4—11 sts.

Row 12 Purl.

Row 13 Bind off 3 sts, k1, yo, k1, yo, k5—10 sts.

Row 14 Bind off 3 sts, p6—7 sts.

Row 15 Ssk, k3, k2 tog—5 sts.

Row 16 Purl.

Row 17 Ssk, k1, k2 tog—3 sts.

Row 18 Purl.

Row 19 Sl 1, k2 tog, psso.

Fasten off.

Large leaf

Cast on 7 sts.

Row 1 (rs) K3, yo, k1, yo, k3—9 sts.

Row 2 Purl.

Row 3 K4, yo, k1, yo, k4—11 sts.

Row 4 Purl.

Row 5 K5, yo, k1, yo, k5—13 sts.

Row 6 Purl.

Row 7 Bind off 3 sts, k2, yo, k1, yo, k6—12 sts.

Row 8 Bind off 3 sts, p8—9 sts.

Row 9 K4, yo, k1, yo, k4—11 sts.

Row 10 Purl.

Row 11 K5, yo, k1, yo, k5—13 sts.

Row 12 Purl.

Row 13 Bind off 3 sts, k2, yo, k1, yo, k6—12 sts.

Row 14 Bind off 3 sts, p8—9 sts.

Row 15 K4, yo, k1, yo, k4—11 sts.

Row 16 Purl.

Row 17 K5, yo, k1, yo, k5—13 sts.

Row 18 Purl.

Row 19 Bind off 3 sts, k9—10 sts.

Row 20 Bind off 3 sts, p6—7 sts.

Row 21 Ssk, k3, k2 tog—5 sts.

Row 22 Purl.

Row 23 Ssk, k1, k2 tog—3 sts.

Row 24 Purl.

Row 25 Sl 1, k2 tog, psso.

Fasten off.

ACORNS (make 2)

With smaller needles and B, cast on 5 sts, leaving long end for seaming.

Row 1 (rs) K in front and back of each st across—10 sts.

Row 2 Purl.

Rows 3-10 Cont in st st as established. Change to A.

Row 11 K1, k into front and back of next 8 sts, k1—18 sts.

Rows 12-16 Knit.

Row 17 K2 tog across—9 sts.

Row 18 [K2 tog] 4 times, k1—5 sts.

Cut yarn, leaving 36-in. end. With tapestry needle, thread end through rem sts on needle.

Gather up and fasten securely. Do not cut. Stuff with small amount of fiberfill. Gather cast-on edge, sew seam, and fasten off.

FINISHING

Sew back seam of hat, reversing first inch for bottom roll. Sew ear flaps in place at each side of hat under bottom roll. Arrange leaves, overlapping them randomly on top of hat, and tack in place. With crochet hook and long end of A at top of each acorn, make chain cord—one 4 in. long and the other 6 in. long. Fasten acorns to top of hat by end of each chain. If desired, tack mid-point of each chain to hat. Weave in all ends.

Beaujolais

This is an easy, quick cap to knit. For the background you can use one to two skeins of yarn left over from a sweater, and for the grapes you can use a small amount of any color yarn. Pin-mark where you want the top and bottom of the grapes to be, then start at the bottom with one grape. Use two grapes for the next level and then three grapes for the next level until you have formed a bunch of grapes. Then top it with a leaf or two. Voilà! Beaujolais that will even improve with age.

SIZE

One size (fits average adult)

MATERIALS

Yarn

Tahki Donegal Tweed, 3½ oz./100 g skein; each about 183 yd./167 m:

- **A** Blue 862—1 skein
- **B** Purple 804—1 skein
- **C** Olive 846—1 skein
- **D** Dark Green 878—1 skein
- **E** Gold 802—1 skein

Needles

- Size 7, or size required to obtain correct gauge
- Size F crochet hook

Other

- Tapestry needle

GAUGE

18 sts and 24 rows = 4 in. in st st
To save time, take time to check the gauge.

NOTES

Stitch counts in the directions include two selvage stitches for seaming.

HAT

With A, cast on 95 sts [93 patt sts + 2 selvage sts].
Work even in st st for 8½ in.; end ws.
Dec row (rs) K1, *k3 tog; rep from * to last st, k1—33 sts.
Work even in st st for 1½ in.
Change to B; cont in st st for 1 in. more.
Bind off.

LEAF

Use colors B, C, and E, changing colors mid-row as desired.
Cast on 7 sts.
Row 1 (rs) K3, yo, k1, yo, k3—9 sts.
Row 2 Purl.
Row 3 K4, yo, k1, yo, k4—11 sts.
Row 4 Purl.
Row 5 K5, yo, k1, yo, k5—13 sts.
Row 6 Purl.
Row 7 Bind off 3 sts, k2, yo, k1, yo, k6—12 sts.
Row 8 Bind off 3 sts, p8—9 sts.
Row 9 K4, yo, k1, yo, k4—11 sts.

Row 10 Purl.

Row 11 K5, yo, k1, yo, k5—13 sts.

Row 12 Purl.

Row 13 Bind off 3 sts, k2, yo, k1, yo, k6—12 sts.

Row 14 Bind off 3 sts, p8—9 sts.

Row 15 K4, yo, k1, yo, k4—11 sts.

Row 16 Purl.

Row 17 K5, yo, k1, yo, k5—13 sts.

Row 18 Purl.

Row 19 Bind off 3 sts, k9—10 sts.

Row 20 Bind off 3 sts, p6—7 sts.

Row 21 Ssk, k3, k2 tog—5 sts.

Row 22 Purl.

Row 23 Ssk, k1, k2 tog—3 sts.

Row 24 Purl.

Row 25 Sl 1, k2 tog, psso.

Fasten off.

GRAPES (*make 19 of B and 1 of C*)

Leave 3-in. tail when casting on and another when fastening off for attaching grapes to hat.

Cast on 1 st.

Row 1 (rs) K5 sts into one st as follows: [k into front, then back of st] twice, then k into front once more before slipping it from needle.

Row 2 P5.

Row 3 K5.

Row 4 P5.

Row 5 K2 tog, k1, k2 tog.

Row 6 P3.

Row 7 Sl 1, k2 tog, psso.

Fasten off.

FINISHING

Sew back seam of hat, reversing first and last inch for top and bottom roll. Referring to photo on p. 8 for placement, tack leaf in place at three or four points.

Attach the grapes by pulling beg and end yarn tails through to ws with crochet hook or tapestry needle. Knot securely on ws and trim ends.

With D, embroider stem st vine, as shown in illustration below. Weave in all ends.

With crochet hook and A, make 20-in.-long chain cord. Thread through openings formed on dec row, knot each end, and tie in a bow, gathering top of hat.

STEM STITCH

Work from left to right, taking regular, slightly slanting stitches along line of design. The thread always emerges on left side of previous stitch.

Berry Nice

This cap begins with a cable rib and goes into reverse stockinette stitch for the background. The crown shaping is a simple knit 2 together decrease. The tube stitch and leaf are worked in one piece. Follow the drawing on p. 18 for placement of the leaves and berries or create your own placement. The knitted tassels are twisted to form corkscrews.

SIZE

Small (medium, large)
Directions are for smallest size, with larger sizes in parentheses. If only one figure appears, it applies to all sizes.

MATERIALS

Yarn

Reynolds Paterna Handknitting Yarn, 1¾ oz./50 g skein; each about 110 yd./100 m:
- **A** Dark Forest 912–1 skein
- **B** Medium Forest 922–1 skein
- **C** Mustard 439–small amount
- **D** Rose 841–small amount
- **E** Burgundy 815–small amount

Needles

- Sizes 5 and 7, or size required to obtain correct gauge
- Cable needle

Other

- Tapestry needle

GAUGE

20 sts and 28 rows = 4 in. in rev st st using larger needles
To save time, take time to check gauge.

NOTES

Stitch counts in the directions include two selvage stitches for seaming.

GLOSSARY

Cable rib: multiple of 6 + 2

Row 1 (rs) P2, *k4, p2; rep from *.
Row 2 K2, *p4, k2; rep from *.
Row 3 P2, *sl next 2 sts to cn and hold to front of work, k2, k2 from cn, p2; rep from *.
Row 4 K2, *p4, k2; rep from *.
Rep rows 1-4 for cable rib.

HAT

With smaller needles and A, cast on 92 (98, 104) sts [90 (96, 102) patt sts + 2 selvage sts].
Work rows 1-4 of cable rib 3 times—approx 1½ in.
Next row (rs) Change to larger needles and work even in rev st st until 8 in. from beg; end rs.

Crown

Dec row 1 (ws) K1, *k2 tog; rep from * to last st, k1—
47 (50, 53) sts.
Dec row 2 P2 (1, 2), *p2 tog; rep from * to last st, p1—
25 (26, 28) sts.
Dec row 3 K2 (1, 1), *k2 tog; rep from * to last st, k1—
14 (14, 15) sts.
Cut yarn, leaving long end. With tapestry needle, thread
end through rem sts on needle.
Gather up and fasten securely.

TUBE ST *(make 6)*

With smaller needles and B, cast on 5 sts.
Row 1 (rs) K1, *sl 1 as if to p, k1; rep from *.
Row 2 Sl 1 as if to p, *p1, sl 1 as if to p; rep from *.
Rep rows 1 and 2 for 2 in.
Bind off.

TUBE ST WITH LEAF *(make 6)*

With smaller needles and B, work tube st for 4 in.
Do not bind off. Cont to make leaf as follows:
Row 1 (rs) K2, yo, k1, yo, k2—7 sts.
Even rows 2-12 Purl.
Row 3 K3, yo, k1, yo, k3—9 sts.
Row 5 K4, yo, k1, yo, k4—11 sts.
Row 7 Ssk, k7, k2 tog—9 sts.
Row 9 Ssk, k5, k2 tog—7 sts.
Row 11 Ssk, k3, k2 tog—5 sts.
Row 13 Ssk, k1, k2 tog—3 sts.
Row 14 (ws) Sl 1, p2 tog, psso—1 st.
Fasten off.

BERRIES *(make 10 each of C, D, and E)*

Leave 3-in. tail when casting on and another when
fastening off for attaching berries to hat.
With smaller needles, cast on 1 st.
Row 1 (rs) K5 sts into one st as follows: [k into front, then
back of st] twice, then k into front once more before
slipping it from needle.
Row 2 P5.
Row 3 K5.
Row 4 P5.
Row 5 K5.
With left needle, pass 2nd, 3rd, 4th, and 5th st on right
needle over first st to complete berry.
Fasten off.

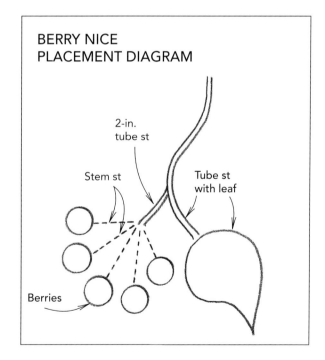

BERRY NICE
PLACEMENT DIAGRAM

2-in.
tube st

Stem st

Tube st
with leaf

Berries

FINISHING

Referring to photo on p. 8 and placement diagram on facing page and starting from top of hat, sew each tube st with attached leaf in place.

Sew six 2-in. lengths of tube st in place, branching off each tube st with attached leaf.

With single strand of B and stem st and referring to illustration on p. 16, embroider 5 stems from end of each 2-in. tube st.

Attach berries, as desired, at end of each stem st arm by pulling beg and end yarn tails through to ws with tapestry needle. Knot securely on ws and trim ends.

Weave in all ends.

Sew back seam of hat.

CORKSCREW TASSELS
(make 1 short and 2 long)

With smaller needles and B, cast on 30 sts for short tassel and 40 sts for long tassel.

Row 1 K into front, then back, then front of each st before slipping it from needle.

Row 2 Bind off in purl.

Attach one end of each tassel at top of hat; weave in yarn tail at rem end. Twist each tassel to form corkscrew.

Grape Harvest

Inspiration for this cap was the sight, smell, and festivities associated with a grape harvest. This self-lined hat is knit in one piece. You start by knitting a 6½-in. self-lining (which later conceals the back of the intarsia, embroidery, and appliqué side). The blank graph on p. 23 has been included for you to create your own designs as simple or as complicated as you like.

SIZE

Small (medium, large)
Directions are for smallest size, with larger sizes in parentheses. If only one figure appears, it applies to all sizes.

MATERIALS

Yarn

Reynolds Paterna Handknitting Yarn, 1¾ oz./50 g skein; each about 110 yd./100 m:
- **A** Dark Burgundy 811–2 skeins
- **B** Medium Brown 412–1 skein
- **C** Light Purple 616–1 skein
- **D** Dark Purple 608–1 skein
- **E** Light Mauve 478–1 skein
- **F** Violet 212–1 skein
- **G** Wine 808–1 skein
- **H** Red 206–1 skein
- **J** Mustard 439–1 skein
- **K** Blue-Green 908–1 skein
- **L** Sage Green 918–1 skein
- **M** Seafoam 928–1 skein
- **N** Olive 917–1 skein

Needles

- Sizes 6 and 7, or size required to obtain correct gauge

Other

- Tapestry needle
- Bobbins

GAUGE

20 sts and 28 rows = 4 in. in st st using larger needles
To save time, take time to check gauge.

NOTES

Stitch counts in the directions and chart include two selvage stitches for seaming.

Read chart on p. 22 from right to left for right side rows and from left to right for wrong side rows.

Use separate bobbin for each block of color. When changing colors, twist yarns on wrong side to prevent holes.

Grape placement is indicated on chart, but grapes are worked separately and then attached to hat.

HAT

With smaller needles and A, cast on 100 (104, 108) sts—[98 (102, 106) patt sts + 2 selvage sts]. Work even in st st for 6½ in. for lining; end rs.
Turning row (ws) Knit.

Omit for medium.

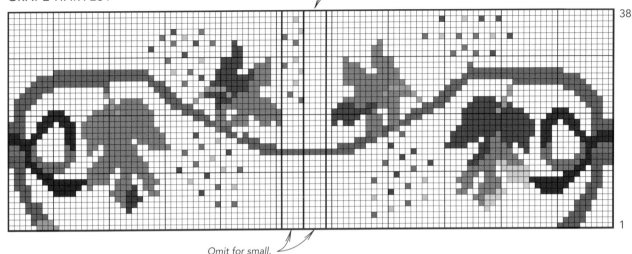

38

1

Omit for small.

Change to larger needles.

K1 row.

P1 row.

Beg chart (rs) Cont in st st work 38 rows of chart, eliminating marked center sts for small and medium sizes. Then work even in st st with A until 6½ in. from turning row; end ws.

Crown

Dec row 1 (rs) K1, *k2 tog; rep from * to last st, k1—51 (53, 55) sts.

Dec row 2 P1, *p2 tog; rep from * to last 2 sts, p2—27 (28, 29) sts.

Dec row 3 K2 (1, 2), *k2 tog; rep from * to last st, k1—15 (15, 16) sts.

Cut yarn, leaving long end. With tapestry needle, thread end through rem sts on needle.

Gather up and fasten securely.

GRAPES *(make 64 for small size and 74 for medium and large sizes)*

Use colors C, D, E, and F as indicated on chart above.

Leave 3-in. tail when casting on and another when fastening off for attaching grapes to hat.

Cast on 1 st.

Row 1 (rs) K5 sts into one st as follows: [k into front, then back of st] twice, then k into front once more before slipping it from needle.

Row 2 P5.

Row 3 K5.

Row 4 P5.

Row 5 K5.

With left needle, pass 2nd, 3rd, 4th, and 5th st on right needle over first st to complete grape.

Fasten off.

Attach grapes by pulling beg and end yarn tails through to ws with tapestry needle. Knot securely on ws and trim ends.

BLANK GRAPH

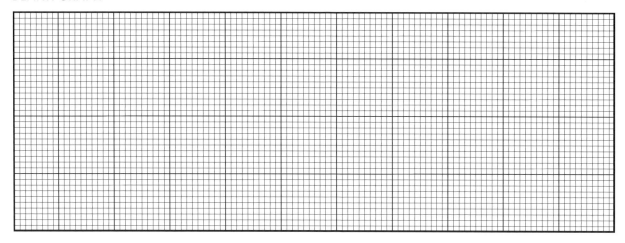

KEY

☐ A

▨ B

░ C GRAPE

░ D GRAPE

▨ E GRAPE

░ F GRAPE

■ G

▨ H

▨ J

▨ K

▨ L

░ M

▨ N

*Create your own design
on this blank graph.*

FINISHING

Referring to photo on p. 20 and illustration on p. 16, work stem st on leaves with single strand of J and on grapevines with single strand of B.

Complete lining

With rs facing and A, pick up and k100 (104, 108) sts across cast-on edge.

Dec row 1 (ws) P2 tog across—50 (52, 54) sts.

Dec row 2 K2 tog across—25 (26, 27) sts.

Dec row 3 P1 (0, 1), *p2 tog; rep from *—13 (13, 14) sts.

Cut yarn, leaving long end. With tapestry needle, thread end through rem sts on needle. Gather up and fasten securely. With separate thread, sew back of hat and lining seams.

With separate thread, gather lining sts and fasten securely. Fold lining into hat at turning row and tack layers together.

Moon Trees

This hat is worked with a variegated background and solid trees (two solid colors can be used). The tree trunks are worked in the rib band and placed on holders, then the trees are picked up and knit separately. After the background is worked (but before the crown shaping), the trees are sewn to the cap. Then the moon is duplicate stitched and the crown shaping is completed.

SIZE
One size (fits average adult)

MATERIALS
Yarn
Stahl Wolle Limbo, 1¾ oz./50 g skein; each about 137 yd./125 m:
- **A** Brown/Green multicolor 2525–2 skeins
- **B** Olive 4520–1 skein
- **C** Gold 4518–small amount

Needles
- Sizes 4 and 5, or size required to obtain correct gauge

Other
- Tapestry needle
- Stitch holders
- Cardboard for pom-pom

GAUGE
24 sts and 30 rows = 4 in. in st st using larger needles
To save time, take time to check gauge.

NOTES
Stitch counts in the directions include two selvage stitches for seaming.

Tree trunks are knit into rib; trees are completed after working hat to crown shaping.

Use separate balls of yarn for each color area on ribbing. When changing colors, twist yarns on wrong side to prevent holes.

HAT
With smaller needles and A, cast on 122 sts [120 patt sts + 2 selvage sts].
Establish k1, p1 rib and color changes for tree trunks (B) as follows:
Row 1 (rs) With A, [k1, p1] 5 times, *rib 7 sts B, rib 17 sts A; rep from *, end last rep rib 9 sts A.
Row 2 Knit the knit sts and purl the purl sts as they face you.
Work even for 1¼ in. in rib patt; end ws.
Change to larger needles and st st, cont with A only.
Next row (rs) *K to tree trunk, place 7 sts of trunk on holder, cast on 7 sts; rep from *, k to end of row after last rep.
Work even in st st for 6 in.; end ws.
Place all sts on a long holder.

TREES *(make 2 large and 3 small)*

Large trees

With rs facing, work large trees over first and third trunk from rh edge of hat as follows:

With smaller needles and B, cast on 8 sts.

Row 1 (rs) K8 cast-on sts, k7 trunk sts from holder, cast on 8 sts—23 sts.

Row 2 and every alt row Purl.

Row 3 K9, ssk, yo, k1, yo, k2 tog, k9—23 sts.

Row 5 K1, ssk, k6, ssk, yo, k1, yo, k2 tog, k6, k2 tog, k1—21 sts.

Row 7 K1, ssk, k5, ssk, yo, k1, yo, k2 tog, k5, k2 tog, k1—19 sts.

Row 9 K1, ssk, k4, ssk, yo, k1, yo, k2 tog, k4, k2 tog, k1—17 sts.

Row 11 K1, ssk, k3, ssk, yo, k1, yo, k2 tog, k3, k2 tog, k1—15 sts.

Row 13 K1, ssk, k2, ssk, yo, k1, yo, k2 tog, k2, k2 tog, k1—13 sts.

Row 15 K1, ssk, k1, ssk, yo, k1, yo, k2 tog, k1, k2 tog, k1—11 sts.

Row 17 Cast on and k5 sts, k3, ssk, yo, k1, yo, k2 tog, k3, cast on 5 sts—21 sts.

Row 19 K1, ssk, k5, ssk, yo, k1, yo, k2 tog, k5, k2 tog, k1—19 sts.

Row 21 K1, ssk, k4, ssk, yo, k1, yo, k2 tog, k4, k2 tog, k1—17 sts.

Row 23 K1, ssk, k3, ssk, yo, k1, yo, k2 tog, k3, k2 tog, k1—15 sts.

Row 25 K1, ssk, k2, ssk, yo, k1, yo, k2 tog, k2, k2 tog, k1—13 sts.

Row 27 K1, ssk, k1, ssk, yo, k1, yo, k2 tog, k1, k2 tog, k1—11 sts.

Row 29 K1, [ssk] twice, yo, k1, yo, [k2 tog] twice, k1—9 sts.

Row 31 Cast on and k3 sts, k2, ssk, yo, k1, yo, k2 tog, k2, cast on 3 sts—15 sts.

Row 33 K1, ssk, k2, ssk, yo, k1, yo, k2 tog, k2, k2 tog, k1—13 sts.

Row 35 K1, ssk, k1, ssk, yo, k1, yo, k2 tog, k1, k2 tog, k1—11 sts.

Row 37 K1, [ssk] twice, yo, k1, yo, [k2 tog] twice, k1—9 sts.

Row 39 K1, ssk, k3, k2 tog, k1—7 sts.

Row 41 K1, ssk, k1, k2 tog, k1—5 sts.

Row 43 Ssk, k1, k2 tog—3 sts.

Row 45 Sl 1, k2 tog, psso.

Fasten off.

Small trees

With rs facing, work small trees over rem trunks as follows:

Work same as for large trees through row 30.

Skip rows 31-38; then complete by working rows 39-45.

Fasten off.

Lightly press all trees. Pin trees in place and sew to hat from front. Sew small slits formed by cast-on sts of A behind each trunk closed.

CROWN

Return sts from long holder to larger needle. Cont in st st with A, dec as follows:

Row 1 (rs) K1, *k2 tog, k1; rep from * k1—82 sts.

Row 2 and every alt row Purl.

Row 3 K1, *k2 tog, k1; rep from *—55 sts.

Row 5 K1, *k2 tog; rep from * to last 2 sts, k2—29 sts.

Row 7 K1, *k2 tog; rep from * to last 2 sts, k2—16 sts.

Cut yarn, leaving long end. With tapestry needle, thread end through rem sts on needle.

Gather up and fasten securely.

FINISHING

Moon

Referring to photo on p. 24 and chart at right, mark area 7 sts wide by 8 rows high with basting thread. With C, work duplicate st following chart.

Sew back seam of hat. Weave in all ends.

Pom-pom (make 1)

Cut two 3¾-in. cardboard circles. Cut a ¾-in. hole in center of each circle. Cut small wedge of each donut shape away to make it easier to wrap yarn. Place circles together. With A, wrap yarn 251 times around donut shape.

Insert scissors between cardboard circles and carefully cut around outer edge to release yarn. Slip a length of yarn between cardboard circles and knot tightly. Gently ease cardboard from pom-pom. Trim to neaten, then fasten to top of hat.

MOON TREES

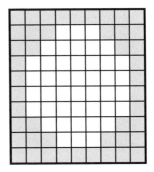

Berets

Berets are forever in style. A beret can be worn many ways, and the way one wears a beret makes an individual statement...from Marlene Dietrich to Charles Boyer to Pepe le Pew. This chapter includes 5-spiral and 10-spiral berets worked on straight needles, a semi-traditional Fair Isle, a straight spoke decrease knit in the round, and my own non-traditional counterpane beret.

To size a beret only the rib band changes—the diameter of a beret top is usually 10 in. to 11 in. and remains the same. To make the beret smaller, eliminate stitches; to make it larger, add stitches. Generally, you should only have to add or decrease a few stitches. Take into consideration your personal increase or decrease count in the sizing when you knit the body of the hat based on my pattern.

Clockwise from top:
St. Pat's Blarney, Mon Chéri, French Scribble

Mon Chéri

This French-inspired hat is worked with a twisted cable rib band and mitered double decreases that form straight lines. Stripe patterns jog when knitting in the round, so on this hat I chose to use I-cord appliquéd on after the hat is knitted. The cherries and leaves were then added. Mon Chéri is my trip to Paris without the passport!

SIZE

One size (fits average adult)

MATERIALS

Yarn

Lane Borgosesia Knitaly, 3½ oz./100 g skein; each about 215 yd./196 m:

- **A** Ecru 2428—1 skein
- **B** Black Nero—1 skein
- **C** Green 2479—small amount
- **D** Red 3793—small amount
- **E** Brown 1366—small amount

Needles

- Sizes 4 and 5 circular, 16 in. long, or size required to obtain correct gauge
- Size 5 double-pointed needles
- Size 5 straight needles for leaves and cherries
- Size F crochet hook

Other

- Tapestry needle
- Stitch markers

GAUGE

22 sts and 30 rnds = 4 in. in st st using larger needle
To save time, take time to check gauge.

GLOSSARY

Twisted cable rib (multiple of 4 sts)

Rnds 1, 2 & 4: *K2, p2; rep from * around.
Rnd 3: *K2 tog but do not sl sts off needle, reinsert needle between these sts and k the first st again, slipping both sts off the needle tog, p2; rep from * around.
Rep rnds 1-4 for rib.

Double dec

Sl 2 sts tog knitwise, k1, pass the 2 sl sts over k st.

I-Cord

With double-pointed needles, cast on 3 sts. *Knit across. Do not turn work. Push the sts back to rh end of needle. Pull to tighten and rep from * until cord measures desired length. Bind off.

HAT

With smaller circular needle and A, cast on 112 sts.
Place cc marker for end of rnd and join, taking care not to twist sts.
Work in twisted cable rib as follows: work rnds 1-4 twice, then rep rnds 1-2.
Change to larger circular needle and k1 rnd, inc 56 sts evenly spaced—168 sts.
Work even in st st until 3¾ in. above rib.
Place markers to divide work evenly into 7 segments of 24 sts each.

Dec rnd 1 *K11, double dec, k10; rep from * over each segment around—154 sts.

Rnd 2 and every alt rnd Purl.

Rnd 3 *K10, double dec, k9; rep from * over each segment around—140 sts.

Rnd 5 *K9, double dec, k8; rep from * over each segment around—126 sts.

Cont to dec over odd-numbered rnds as established. Each succeeding rnd will have two less sts per segment. Change to double-pointed needles when necessary. When 14 sts rem work final rnd as follows:

Final rnd *K2 tog; rep from *—7 sts.

Cut yarn, leaving long end. With tapestry needle, thread end through rem sts on needle. Gather up and fasten securely.

Block hat over 11-in. plate.

LEAVES (make 14 of C)

With straight needles, cast on 5 sts. Work back and forth in rows as follows:

Row 1 (rs) K2, yo, k1, yo, k2—7 sts.

Even rows 2-8 Purl.

Row 3 K3, yo, k1, yo, k3—9 sts.

Row 5 Ssk, k5, k2 tog—7 sts.

Row 7 Ssk, k3, k2 tog—5 sts.

Row 9 Ssk, k1, k2 tog—3 sts.

Row 10 P3 tog.

Fasten off.

CHERRIES (make 14)

With straight needles and a double strand of D, cast on 1 st.

Row 1 (rs) K5 sts into one st as follows: [k into front, then back of st] twice, then k into front once more before slipping it from needle.

Row 2 P5.

Row 3 K5.

Row 4 P5.

Row 5 K2 tog, k1, k2 tog.

Row 6 P3 tog.

Fasten off. Knot beg and end yarn ends tog and tuck into cherry.

With crochet hook, attach E to cherry. Chain 9 for short stems on 7 cherries; chain 12 for long stems on 7 rem cherries.

Fasten off stems, leaving 3-in. tail for attaching to hat.

FINISHING

Referring to photo on p. 28, with scrap yarn baste 4 circles evenly spaced on top of hat to mark I-cord trim placement.

With B, make a length of I-cord to fit over each circle.

With rs facing, baste or pin I-cord in place. With rs facing and with tapestry needle and B, secure by catching center sts at base of I-cord with running sts.

Remove basting.

Tack 7 pairs of leaves evenly spaced between the two outermost circles of I-cord (see photo on p. 28).

Attach one short- and one long-stemmed cherry at the base of each pair of leaves by pulling stem tails through to ws with crochet hook or tapestry needle. Fasten securely on ws.

Weave in all ends.

French Scribble

This is a basic 10-spiral beret worked like the 5-spiral beret (Hugs 'n Kisses on p. 37) but with a knit 2 together decrease. The scribble is worked with I-cord, which is sewn on after the hat has been knitted and blocked.

SIZE

One size (fits average adult)

MATERIALS

Yarn

Reynolds Lite-Lopi, 1¾ oz./50 g skein; each about 109 yd./100 m:
- **A** Red 0434—2 skeins
- **B** Black 0059—1 skein

Needles

- Sizes 4 and 5, or size required to obtain correct gauge
- Size 5 double-pointed needles

Other

- Tapestry needle

GAUGE

20 sts and 24 rows = 4 in. in st st using larger needles
To save time, take time to check gauge.

NOTES

Stitch counts in the directions do not include two selvage stitches for seaming unless otherwise noted.

GLOSSARY

I-Cord

With double-pointed needles, cast on 3 sts. *Knit across. Do not turn work. Push the sts back to rh end of needle. Pull to tighten and rep from * until cord measures desired length. Bind off.

HAT

With smaller needles and A, cast on 102 sts [100 patt sts + 2 selvage sts].
Work in k1, p1 rib for 1¼ in.
Change to larger needles and st st.
Row 1 (rs) *Inc in next st, k9; rep from *—110 sts.
Row 2 and every alt row Purl.
Row 3 *Inc in next st, k10; rep from *—120 sts.
Row 5 *Inc in next st, k11; rep from *—130 sts.
Row 7 *Inc in next st, k12; rep from *—140 sts.
Row 9 *Inc in next st, k13; rep from *—150 sts.
Row 11 *Inc in next st, k14; rep from *—160 sts.
Beg on ws, work even in st st for 5 rows; then work dec rows as follows:
Dec row 1 (rs) *K2 tog, k14; rep from *—150 sts.

Row 2 and every alt row Purl.

Row 3 *K2 tog, k13; rep from *—140 sts.

Row 5 *K2 tog, k12; rep from *—130 sts.

Row 7 *K2 tog, k11; rep from *—120 sts.

Row 9 *K2 tog, k10; rep from *—110 sts.

Row 11 *K2 tog, k9; rep from *—100 sts.

Row 13 *K2 tog, k8; rep from *—90 sts.

Row 15 *K2 tog, k7; rep from *—80 sts.

Row 17 *K2 tog, k6; rep from *—70 sts.

Row 19 *K2 tog, k5; rep from *—60 sts.

Row 21 *K2 tog, k4; rep from *—50 sts.

Row 23 *K2 tog, k3; rep from *—40 sts.

Row 25 *K2 tog, k2; rep from *—30 sts.

Row 27 *K2 tog, k1; rep from *—20 sts.

Row 29 *K2 tog; rep from *—10 sts.

Row 30 Purl.

Cut yarn, leaving long end. With tapestry needle, thread end through rem sts on needle.

Gather up and fasten securely.

FINISHING

Sew back seam. Weave in all ends.

Block over 11-in. plate.

With double-pointed needles and B, work a length of I-cord about 7 ft. long. Do not bind off.

Referring to photo on p. 28, baste cord in place, forming one loop over each of the 10 inc/dec sections of the hat. Adjust length of cord by ripping back or working additional length to fit. Fasten off.

With rs facing, catch center sts at base of cord with running sts to secure.

St. Pat's Blarney

This traditional Fair Isle pattern is my tribute to the Irish. I start with a blue ocean and sparkle it with blue metallic yarn and white wave tops, then continue with green and ocean sand. Then I top it off with the last snake that St. Patrick drove into the Irish sea. Instructions are given for an optional tubular cast-on that can be used on other hats in place of a regular cast-on. (It's a matter of personal preference.) Note: Two hats can be completed with the yarn amount that you need to purchase for one hat.

SIZE

One size (fits average adult)

MATERIALS

Yarn

Rowan Donegal Lambswool Tweed, 1 oz./25 g skein, each about 109 yd./100 m:

- **A** Sapphire 486—1 skein
- **B** Dolphin 478—1 skein
- **C** Juniper 482—1 skein
- **D** Bay 485—1 skein
- **E** Leaf 481—1 skein
- **F** Oatmeal 469—1 skein
- **G** Ivory 465— 1 skein

Metallic yarn, sport wt.:

- **H** Dark blue—small amount
- **I** Gold—small amount
- **J** Green—small amount

Needles
- Sizes 1 and 3 circular, 16 in. long, or size required to obtain correct gauge
- Size 3 double-pointed needles

Other
- Tapestry needle
- Stitch markers
- 2 small green sequins for snake's eyes
- For optional tubular cast-on and rib, you will also need waste yarn and ravel cord or waxed cotton yarn.

GAUGE

28 sts and 43 rnds = 4 in. in st st using larger needle
To save time, take time to check gauge.

NOTES

Metallic yarn is always worked held together with one strand of Donegal Lambswool Tweed as indicated in directions with the exception of Gold (I) highlights that occur in Wheel and Bar chart. These stitches are indicated by red outline and are worked in duplicate stitch over charted color when hat is completed.

When stranding yarns, pick up colors alternately over and under one another. Where long floats (more than 4 or 5 stitches) of any one color occur, twist them around the working yarn on wrong side every few stitches as necessary.

Read Charts 1-4 on p. 36 from right to left, bottom to top every round. Read Wheel and Bar chart on p. 36 as indicated in directions.

Both conventional and tubular cast-on and rib variations are given. Select the one that best suits you.

GLOSSARY
Double dec
Sl 2 sts tog knitwise, k1, pass the 2 sl sts over k st.

HAT
Conventional cast on and rib
With smaller circular needle and A, cast on 144 sts.
Place marker for end of rnd and join, taking care not to twist sts.
Work in k1, p1 rib for 1 in.

Tubular cast on and rib
With larger circular needle and waste yarn, cast on 72 sts.
K1 row with ravel cord or waxed cotton yarn; then divide sts evenly onto 4 double-pointed needles.
Place cc marker on the end of the last needle to mark the end of the rnd.
Join, being careful not to twist sts.
Change to color A; then *k1, yo; rep from * around— 144 sts.
Rnds 1 & 3 *K1, wyif, sl 1 purlwise, yarn back; rep from * to marker.
Rnds 2 & 4 *Wyib, sl 1 purlwise, yarn forward, p1; rep from * to marker.
Change to smaller circular needle.
Rnd 5 *K1, p1; rep from * to marker.
Rep rnd 5 until 1 in. from rnd 1.
When rib is completed, pull on ravel cord or waxed cotton yarn to remove it from base of hat, along with waste yarn.

Cont with hat as follows

Change to larger needle and k1 rnd, inc 36 sts evenly spaced—180 sts.

Cont in st st throughout.

Beg Chart 1

Rnds 1-5 Use 1 strand of H held tog with B.

Rnds 6-10 Work as charted.

Beg Chart 2

Rnds 1-4 Work as charted.

Beg Chart 3

Rnds 1-4 Work as charted.

Rnds 5-7 Use 1 strand of H held tog with C.

Rnds 8-11 Work as charted.

Beg Chart 4

Rnds 1-3 Use 1 strand of H held tog with A.

Next rnd With G, inc 2 sts evenly placed over rnd—182 sts.

Beg Wheel and Bar chart

Place markers to divide work evenly into 7 segments of 26 sts each.

Rep Wheel and Bar chart as follows over each of the 7 segments:

General *Always beg chart at center of pie-shaped section at arrow. Read from arrow to left edge, then from bar at right edge back across right side of pie-shaped section to arrow; rep from * for each segment around.

For rnds where a dec is indicated by one less st at both edges of pie-shaped section of chart *Work from center to left edge of chart, sl next 2 sts tog knitwise (1 of the sts to be dec and the st from the bar at right edge of chart), knit next st (the other st to be dec), pass the 2 slipped sts over the k1 (1 double dec made—the st slipped from the bar appears as the visible st of the double dec); complete rep from right edge of pie-shaped chart back to arrow; rep from * for each segment around.

Rnds 1 & 2 Work as charted.

Rnds 3-7 Use 1 strand of J held tog with D.

Rnd 8 Work as charted.

Rnd 9 Use 1 strand of J held tog with E.

Rnds 10-25 Work as charted, changing to double-pointed needles when necessary.

After Wheel and Bar chart is completed, 14 sts rem.

Final rnd With E, k2 tog around—7 sts.

Do not fasten off.

SNAKE

Cont in rnds on 7 rem sts, working stripes as follows:

Rnds 1-6 Knit with E.

Rnd 7 Knit with E + I held tog.

Rnds 8-11 Knit with E.

Rnds 12-15 Knit with D.

Rnds 16-21 Knit with E.

Rnds 22-25 Knit with E + J held tog.

Rnds 26-29 Knit with E.

Rnds 30-33 Knit with E + I held tog.

Rnds 34-37 Knit with E.

Rnds 38-41 Knit with E + J held tog.

SNAKE'S HEAD

Change to D and work back and forth in rows of st st for ½ in. Then, dec 1 st each side every other row twice.

Next row Sl 1, k2 tog, psso.

Fasten off.

FINISHING

With I, duplicate st highlights over each st of Wheel and Bar chart outlined in red.

Weave in all ends.

Block over 11-in. plate.

Sew sequins in place for snake's eyes.

Referring to photo below, turn snake's body once and sew head in place.

With I, embroider tongue with 2 straight sts.

ST. PAT'S BLARNEY

Chart 1

Chart 3

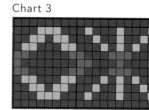

Chart 2

Chart 4

Wheel and Bar Chart

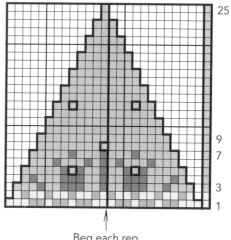

Beg each rep

KEY

☐ Decreased sts—skip when reading Wheel and Bar chart

■ **A** Sapphire

▨ **B** Dolphin

▨ **C** Juniper

▨ **D+J** Bay, Green metallic

▨ **E** Leaf

▨ **F** Oatmeal

☐ **G** Ivory

☐ **I** Gold

■ **A+H** Sapphire, Dark blue metallic

■ **B+H** Dolphin, Dark blue metallic

■ **C+H** Juniper, Dark blue metallic

▨ **E+J** Leaf, Green metallic

Hugs 'n Kisses

This basic 5-spiral beret is worked with a double decrease and one color. The motif is worked in duplicate stitch after the hat is made (see photo on p. 38). The hugs and kisses (Xs and Os) were inspired by the popular jewelry currently in vogue. Once again, you can make a graph to create your own personal touches.

SIZE
One size (fits average adult)

MATERIALS

Yarn
Lion Brand AL-PA-KA, 1¾ oz./50 g skein; each about 107 yd./98 m:
- **A** Black 153–2 skeins

Metallic yarn, sport wt.:
- **B** Silver—small amount
- **C** Gold—small amount

Needles
- Sizes 5 and 7, or size required to obtain correct gauge

Other
- Tapestry needle

GAUGE
20 sts and 24 rows = 4 in. in st st using larger needles
To save time, take time to check gauge.

NOTES
Stitch counts in the directions do not include two selvage stitches for seaming unless otherwise noted.

Motifs are worked in duplicate stitch after hat is completed.

HAT
With smaller needles and A, cast on 102 sts [100 patt sts + 2 selvage sts].
Work in k2, p2 rib for 1 in.; end ws.
Change to larger needles and st st.
Row 1 (rs) *Inc in next st, k9; rep from *—110 sts.
Row 2 and every alt row (ws) Purl.
Row 3 *Inc in next st, k10; rep from *—120 sts.
Row 5 *Inc in next st, k11; rep from *—130 sts.
Row 7 *Inc in next st, k12; rep from *—140 sts.
Row 9 *Inc in next st, k13; rep from *—150 sts.
Row 11 *Inc in next st, k14; rep from *—160 sts.

Beg on ws, work even in st st for 5 rows; then work dec rows as follows:

Dec row 1 (rs) *Sl 1 knitwise, k2 tog, psso, k29; rep from *—150 sts.

Row 2 and every alt row Purl.

Row 3 *Sl 1 knitwise, k2 tog, psso, k27; rep from *—140 sts.

Row 5 *Sl 1 knitwise, k2 tog, psso, k25; rep from *—130 sts.

Row 7 *Sl 1 knitwise, k2 tog, psso, k23; rep from *—120 sts.

Row 9 *Sl 1 knitwise, k2 tog, psso, k21; rep from *—110 sts.

Row 11 *Sl 1 knitwise, k2 tog, psso, k19; rep from *—100 sts.

Row 13 *Sl 1 knitwise, k2 tog, psso, k17; rep from *—90 sts.

Row 15 *Sl 1 knitwise, k2 tog, psso, k15; rep from *—80 sts.

Row 17 *Sl 1 knitwise, k2 tog, psso, k13; rep from *—70 sts.

Row 19 *Sl 1 knitwise, k2 tog, psso, k11; rep from *—60 sts.

Row 21 *Sl 1 knitwise, k2 tog, psso, k9; rep from *—50 sts.

Row 23 *Sl 1 knitwise, k2 tog, psso, k7; rep from *—40 sts.

Row 25 *Sl 1 knitwise, k2 tog, psso, k5; rep from *—30 sts.

Row 27 *Sl 1 knitwise, k2 tog, psso, k3; rep from *—20 sts.

Row 29 *Sl 1 knitwise, k2 tog, psso, k1; rep from *—10 sts.

Row 30 Purl.

Cut yarn, leaving long end. With tapestry needle, thread end through rem sts on needle.

Gather up and fasten securely.

FINISHING

Sew back seam. Weave in all ends.

Block over 11-in. plate.

Referring to photo on facing page and chart below, duplicate st "X O" motif centered over each of the 5 sections of hat.

HUGS 'N KISSES

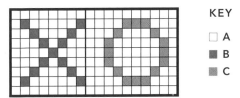

KEY

☐ A
■ B
■ C

Last Leaf

If you've read Melanie Falick's beautiful book Knitting in America, *you'll recognize this design, which is based on my sweater design in that book. I actually had 4 triangles and a few leaves left over from that sweater, and they became the basis for this design. I sewed the triangles together to make the counterpane square and with a circular needle picked up around the edge of the square and worked the rib band. When blocking, I folded the corners to the band and added a few leaves. A unique beret was born from the leftovers, but you'll have to start from scratch with my instructions.*

SIZE

One size (fits average adult)

MATERIALS

Yarn

Rowan DK Tweed, 1¾ oz./50 g skein; each about 119 yd./109 m:
- **A** Cricket 851–2 skeins

Rowan Lightweight DK, 1 oz./25 g skein; each about 73 yd./67 m:
- **B** Rust 71–small amount
- **C** Teal 655–small amount
- **D** Gold 11–small amount
- **E** Light gold 10–small amount

Needles

- Size 4, or size required to obtain correct gauge
- Size 3 circular, 16 in. long

Other

- Tapestry needle
- Stitch marker

GAUGE

One triangle = 5½ in. from longest (bound-off) edge to point using size 4 needles
To save time, take time to check gauge.

NOTES

Main part of hat is made in 4 triangles, which are then sewn together and finished with circular ribbing and appliquéd leaves and berries.

GLOSSARY

Bobble

Row 1 K4 sts into the next st as follows: [K into front, then back of st] twice before slipping it from needle; turn.
Row 2 [K2 tog] twice, turn.
Row 3 K2 tog, cont across row as indicated.

HAT

Triangle (make 4)

With straight needles and A, cast on 1 st.

Row 1 (rs) K into front, then back of st.

Row 2 K1, k into front, then back of last st.

Row 3 K2, k into front, then back of last st.

Rows 4-12 Cont as established, knitting all stitches and working inc (k into front, then back of last st) at end of row—13 sts at end of row 12.

Row 13 K12, k into front, then back of last st.

Row 14 P13, p into back, then front of last st.

Row 15 K14, k into front, then back of last st.

Row 16 P15, p into back, then front of last st.

Row 17 [K2, p2] 4 times, k into front, then back of last st.

Row 18 [P2, k2] 4 times, p1, k into front, then back of last st.

Row 19 P1, [k2, p2] 4 times, k1, k into front, then back of last st.

Row 20 K1, [P2, k2] 4 times, p2, k into front, then back of last st.

Row 21 [P2, k2] 5 times, k into front, then back of last st.

Row 22 P21, p into back, then front of last st.

Row 23 K22, k into front, then back of last st.

Row 24 P23, p into back, then front of last st.

Row 25 K24, k into front, then back of last st.

Row 26 K25, k into front, then back of last st.

Row 27 K26, k into front, then back of last st.

Row 28 K27, k into front, then back of last st.

Row 29 K28, k into front, then back of last st.

Row 30 K29, k into front, then back of last st.

Row 31 K30, k into front, then back of last st.

Row 32 P31, p into back, then front of last st.

Row 33 K32, k into front, then back of last st.

Row 34 K33, k into front, then back of last st.

Row 35 K2, [yo, k2 tog] 16 times, k into front, then back of last st.

Row 36 K35, k into front, then back of last st.

Row 37 K36, k into front, then back of last st.

Row 38 P37, p into back, then front of last st.

Row 39 K2, [bobble, k4] 7 times, bobble, k into front, then back of last st.

Row 40 P39, p into back, then front of last st.

Row 41 K40, k into front, then back of last st.

Row 42 K41, k into front, then back of last st.

Row 43 K2, [yo, k2 tog] 20 times, k into front, then back of last st.

Row 44 K43, k into front, then back of last st.

Row 45 K44, k into front, then back of last st.

Row 46 P45, p into back, then front of last st.

Row 47 K46, k into front, then back of last st.

Row 48 K47, k into front, then back of last st.

Row 49 K48, k into front, then back of last st.

Row 50 K49, k into front, then back of last st.

Row 51 K50, k into front, then back of last st.

Row 52 K51, k into front, then back of last st.

Row 53 Bind off, leaving long end for sewing.

LEAVES (make 3)

Use colors B, C, D, and E and larger needles, changing colors midrow as desired.

Cast on 5 sts.

Row 1 (rs) K2, yo, k1, yo, k2—7 sts.

Row 2 Purl.

Row 3 K3, yo, k1, yo, k3—9 sts.

Row 4 Purl.

Row 5 K4, yo, k1, yo, k4—11 sts.

Row 6 Purl.

Row 7 Bind off 3 sts, k1, yo, k1, yo, k5—10 sts.

Row 8 Bind off 3 sts, p6—7 sts.

Row 9 K3, yo, k1, yo, k3—9 sts.

Row 10 Purl.

Row 11 K4, yo, k1, yo, k4—11 sts.

Row 12 Purl.

Row 13 Bind off 3 sts, k1, yo, k1, yo, k5—10 sts.

Row 14 Bind off 3 sts, p6—7 sts.

Row 15 Ssk, k3, k2 tog—5 sts.

Row 16 Purl.

Row 17 Ssk, k1, k2 tog—3 sts.

Row 18 Purl.

Row 19 Sl 1, k2 tog, psso.

Fasten off.

BERRIES (make 2 of B and 1 of D)

Leave 3-in. tail when casting on and fastening off for attaching berries to hat.

With straight needles, cast on 1 st.

Row 1 (ws) K5 sts into one st as follows: [K into front, then back of st] twice, then k into front once more before slipping it from needle.

Row 2 (rs) P5.

Row 3 K5.

Row 4 P5.

Row 5 K5.

With left needle, pass 2nd, 3rd, 4th, and 5th st on right needle over first st to complete berry.

Fasten off.

FINISHING

Sew 4 triangles together to form a square.

With rs facing and with circular needle and A, pick up and k100 sts evenly spaced around assembled square. Place marker for end of rnd.

Work in k2, p2 rib for 1½ in. Bind off in rib.

Block over 10-in. plate.

Referring to photo on p. 40, arrange berries and 2 leaves at center top of hat and sew in place. Sew rem leaf at corner of square.

Tack each point of top square to rib.

Brim Hats

If you ask five different people (and believe me, I have) what style of hat this is, you're likely to get five different answers. The brim says different things to different people. In this chapter I've included a rolled brim, a visor, a folded leopard brim, a scalloped brim, and a hat titled "Chameleon" that folds to make five different looks. You may think of a sixth or seventh!

Clockwise from top:
Leopard, Bow Jest, Derby

Derby

The polyester-fiberfill rolled brim makes this a really comfy-cozy hat. I've kept it simple, but don't hesitate to add a feather, flower, buttons, embroidery, or color work to make it truly yours. Ribbon can be used for the band.

SIZE

One size (fits average adult)

MATERIALS

Yarn

Crystal Palace Cotton Chenille, 1¾ oz./50 g skein; each about 98 yd./90 m:

- **A** Brown 6262—2 skeins
- **B** Black 9598—small amount

Needles

- Sizes 5 and 6, or size required to obtain correct gauge

Other

- Tapestry needle
- Polyester fiberfill batting: 20-in. by 28-in. piece

GAUGE

18 sts and 24 rows = 4 in. in st st using larger needles
To save time, take time to check gauge.

NOTES

Stitch counts in the directions include two selvage stitches for seaming.

HAT

Brim

With larger needles and A, cast on 96 sts—[94 patt sts + 2 selvage sts].
K1 row.
P1 row.
Next row (rs) Knit, inc 24 sts evenly spaced across— 120 sts.
Work even in st st as established for 5½ in.; end ws.
Next row (rs) Knit, dec 24 sts evenly spaced across— 96 sts.

Side section

Change to smaller needles and work in k1, p1 rib for 1 in.; end ws.
Change to larger needles.
Next row (rs) Knit, dec 4 sts evenly spaced across— 92 sts.
Work even in st st for 3 in.; end ws.

Crown

Row 1 (rs) K1, *k8, k2 tog; rep from *, end k1—83 sts.

Row 2 and every alt row Purl.

Row 3 K1, *k7, k2 tog; rep from *, end k1—74 sts.

Row 5 K1, *k6, k2 tog; rep from *, end k1—65 sts.

Row 7 K1, *k5, k2 tog; rep from *, end k1—56 sts.

Row 9 K1, *k4, k2 tog; rep from *, end k1—47 sts.

Row 11 K1, *k3, k2 tog; rep from *, end k1—38 sts.

Row 13 K1, *k2, k2 tog; rep from *, end k1—29 sts.

Row 15 K1, *k2 tog; rep from *—15 sts.

Cut yarn, leaving long end. With tapestry needle, thread end through rem sts on needle.

Gather up and fasten securely.

Band

With smaller needles and B, cast on 7 sts.

Work in k1, p1 rib for 22 in.

Bind off.

FINISHING

Sew crown, back, and brim seam.

Roll batting into a tight tube beg at long side. Take cast-on edge of brim to inside of hat over tube of batting. Sew cast-on edge of brim to beg of rib section.

Weave ends of band tog; sew band to hat (see photo on p. 44). Weave in all ends.

Bow Jest

This is basically a beret-shaped top with a visor brim that makes it a cap. It has popped up over and over since the '60s. I'll probably design a plutonium one for the year 2000. Leave off the brim and it becomes a beret, or make it multicolored, put a button or pom-pom on top, and call it any kind of hat you want.

SIZE

One size (fits average adult)

MATERIALS

Yarn

Reynolds Paterna Handknitting Yarn, 1¾ oz./50 g skein; each about 110 yd./100 m:
- **A** Black 050—1 skein
- **B** Lime Green 914—1 skein

Needles
- Sizes 5 and 7, or size required to obtain correct gauge

Other
- Tapestry needle

GAUGE

20 sts and 28 rows = 4 in. in st st using larger needles

To save time, take time to check gauge.

NOTES

Stitch counts in the directions do not include two selvage stitches for seaming unless otherwise noted.

Use separate balls of yarn for each color area. When changing colors, twist yarns on wrong side to prevent holes.

When working visor, remember to wrap yarn on short rows to prevent holes.

HAT

With smaller needles and A, cast on 106 sts [104 patt sts + 2 sts for selvages].

Maintain selvage sts throughout hat shaping.

Work in k1, p1 rib for 1½ in.; end ws.

Change to larger needles and st st.

Inc row (rs) Knit, inc 52 sts evenly spaced across—156 sts.

Next row (ws) Establish color segments as follows: *P26 B, p26 A; rep from * across for a total of 6 color segments. Maintain color changes as established throughout.

Work 8 rows even.

Shape top

Row 1 (rs) [With A, ssk, k22, k2 tog; with B, ssk, k22, k2 tog] 3 times—144 sts.

Even rows 2-32 Purl.

Row 3 Knit.

Row 5 [With A, ssk, k20, k2 tog; with B, ssk, k20, k2 tog] 3 times—132 sts.

Row 7 [With A, ssk, k18, k2 tog; with B, ssk, k18, k2 tog] 3 times—120 sts.

Row 9 Knit.

Row 11 [With A, ssk, k16, k2 tog; with B, ssk, k16, k2 tog] 3 times—108 sts.

Row 13 [With A, ssk, k14, k2 tog; with B, ssk, k14, k2 tog] 3 times—96 sts.

Row 15 Knit.

Row 17 [With A, ssk, k12, k2 tog; with B, ssk, k12, k2 tog] 3 times—84 sts.

Row 19 [With A, ssk, k10, k2 tog; with B, ssk, k10, k2 tog] 3 times—72 sts.

Row 21 Knit.

Row 23 [With A, ssk, k8, k2 tog; with B, ssk, k8, k2 tog] 3 times—60 sts.

Row 25 [With A, ssk, k6, k2 tog; with B, ssk, k6, k2 tog] 3 times—48 sts.

Row 27 Knit.

Row 29 [With A, ssk, k4, k2 tog; with B, ssk, k4, k2 tog] 3 times—36 sts.

Row 31 [With A, ssk, k2, k2 tog; with B, ssk, k2, k2 tog] 3 times—24 sts.

Row 33 [With A, ssk, k2 tog; with B, ssk, k2 tog] 3 times—12 sts.

Row 34 P2 tog across—6 sts.

Cut yarn, leaving long end. With tapestry needle, thread end through rem sts on needle.

Gather up and fasten securely.

Visor

With smaller needles and A, cast on 55 sts.

Row 1 Work in k1, p1 rib.

Begin short row shaping as follows:

Row 2 Rib to last 3 sts, slip next st on left needle to right needle, wrap this st, and slip it back to left needle; turn.

Row 3 Rep row 2.

Rows 4-9 Cont as for last 2 rows, leaving 3 more sts unworked at end of every row.

Row 10 Rib to end of row, hiding wraps by knitting or purling them tog with sts they're wrapped around.

Row 11 Rib over all sts, hiding rem wraps.

Bind off in rib.

FINISHING

Sew back seam.

Block cap section over 10-in. plate. Sew visor to cap at center front.

Weave in all ends.

Bow

With smaller needles and B, cast on 15 sts.

Work in k1, p1 rib for 3½ in. Bind off.

With smaller needles and B, cast on 3 sts.

Work in k1, p1 rib for 1½ in. Bind off.

Gather larger strip at center then sew smaller strip around it for "knot."

Referring to photo on p. 44, attach to hat at center front above visor.

Leopard

This hat is an exaggerated pillbox with a leopard brim. You can shorten or lengthen the crown height to your taste without altering the leopard chart. If you're not into leopard spots, you can chart your own design or make it a solid color.

SIZE

One size (fits average adult)

MATERIALS

Yarn

Reynolds Paterna Handknitting Yarn, 1¾ oz./50 g skein; each about 110 yd./100 m:

- **A** Black 050—3 skeins   ARAN
- **B** Light Gold 472—1 skein
- **C** Rust 847—1 skein

Needles

- Sizes 7 and 8, or size required to obtain correct gauge

Other

- Tapestry needle
- Stiffening material: 10-in. square buckram

GAUGE

19 sts and 24 rows = 4 in. in st st using larger needles
To save time, take time to check gauge.

NOTES

Stitch counts in the directions do not include two selvage stitches for seaming unless otherwise noted.

Read chart from right to left for right side rows and from left to right for wrong side rows.

When stranding yarns, pick up colors alternately over and under one another. Where long floats (more than 4 or 5 stitches) of any one color occur, twist them around the working yarn at the wrong side every few stitches as necessary.

Hat is self-lined; instructions begin with lining.

HAT

With smaller needles and A, cast on 102 sts [100 patt sts + 2 selvage sts].

Maintain selvage sts throughout.

Work even in st st for 5½ in. for lining; end ws.

Beg chart (rs) Change to larger needles and cont in st st, work 25-st rep of chart 4 times.

When 12 rows of chart are completed, cont with A as follows:

K2 rows for turning ridge, then work even in st st for 7½ in.; end rs.

K2 rows.

P1 row.

LEOPARD

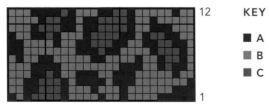

12

1

25-st rep

KEY

■ A
▨ B
■ C

Crown

Row 1 (rs) *K2 tog, k8; rep from *—90 sts.

Row 2 and every alt row Purl.

Row 3 Knit.

Row 5 *K2 tog, k7; rep from *—80 sts.

Row 7 *K2 tog, k6; rep from *—70 sts.

Row 9 *K2 tog, k5; rep from *—60 sts.

Row 11 *K2 tog, k4; rep from *—50 sts.

Row 13 *K2 tog, k3; rep from *—40 sts.

Row 15 *K2 tog, k2; rep from *—30 sts.

Row 17 *K2 tog, k1; rep from *—20 sts.

Row 19 *K2 tog; rep from *—10 sts.

Row 21 *K2 tog; rep from *—5 sts.

Cut yarn, leaving long end. With tapestry needle, thread end through rem sts on needle.

Gather up and fasten securely.

Crown lining

With smaller needles and A, cast on 102 sts [100 patt sts + 2 selvage sts].

Shape as for crown; maintain selvage sts throughout.

FINISHING

Sew crown and back seam. Sew crown lining seam.

Trace crown lining on buckram and cut just inside traced line. Position buckram between crown and crown lining; tack lining in place.

Sew cast-on edge of lining to beg of crown.

Referring to photo on p. 44, fold leopard patt to outside to form brim.

Chameleon

Instructions are given for straight and circular knitting. The pattern stitch used is reversible, lending flexibility to the way the brim is folded for variations of wearing style. The alpaca yarn I've recommended lends itself to the elasticity of the hat. You can use another quality yarn in place of it, but I recommend you stay away from cotton, linen, and other less-resilient yarns that do not maintain their body.

SIZE

One size (fits average adult)

MATERIALS

Yarn

Stacy Charles Filitura di Crosa Alpaca Oggi,
1¾ oz./50 g skein; each about 82 yd./75 m:
- Pink 227 *or* Periwinkle 228 *or* Blue 211 *or* Navy 3 *or* Gray 204 *or* Teal 220—3 skeins

Needles

- Size 8 straight needles if knitting back and forth
- Size 8 circular needle, 16 in. long, if knitting in the round
- Size 8 double-pointed needles, if knitting in the round

Other

- Tapestry needle
- Marker if knitting in the round

GAUGE

16 sts = 3 in. and 30 rows/rnds = 4 in. in patt st
To save time, take time to check gauge.

NOTES

Cast on 1 selvage stitch for seaming at very beginning and end of work if using straight needles; omit selvage stitches if knitting in the round.

Stitch counts in the directions include selvage stitches only as noted for working on straight needles.

GLOSSARY

**Reversible Diagonal Rib Patt
(multiple of 8 sts)**
Row/rnd 1 *K1, p1, k1, p5; rep from *.
Row/rnd 2 and every alt row/rnd Knit the knit sts and purl the purl sts as they face you.
Row/rnd 3 K1, p1, *k5, p1, k1, p1; rep from *, end k5, p1.
Row/rnd 5 K1, *p5, k1, p1, k1; rep from *, end p5, k1, p1.
Row/rnd 7 *K5, p1, k1, p1; rep from *.
Row/rnd 9 P4, *k1, p1, k1, p5; rep from *, end [k1, p1] twice.
Row/rnd 11 K3, *p1, k1, p1, k5; rep from *, end p1, k1, p1, k2.
Row/rnd 13 P2, *k1, p1, k1, p5; rep from *, end k1, p1, k1, p3.
Row/rnd 15 K1, * p1, k1, p1, k5; rep from *, end p1, k1, p1, k4.
Row 16 Knit the knit sts and purl the purl sts as they face you.
Rep rows/rnds 1-16 for patt.

Clockwise from top:
Basic fold hat with pom-pom, Robin Hood, rolled-brim hat,
cloche, miller's hat with hanging pom-pom

HAT

Cast on 104 sts if in the round.

Cast on 106 sts [104 patt sts + 2 sts for selvages] if on straight needles.

Maintaining selvage sts if working straight, work even in Reversible Diagonal Rib Patt for 9 in.; end row 16 of st patt. Then cont with crown shaping as follows:

Crown

Row/rnd 1 *K1, p1, k1, p1, [k2 tog] twice, rep from *— 78 sts. Change to double-pointed needles when necessary.

Rows/rnds 2 & 4 Knit the knit sts and purl the purl sts as they face you.

Row 3 K1, *p1, k1, p1, k3 tog; rep from *, ending last rep k2 tog—53 sts.

Rnd 3 Remove marker. Sl 1, replace marker to reestablish beg of rnd, *p1, k1, p1, k3 tog; rep from *—52 sts.

Rows/rnds 5-9 Work even in rib as established.

For working back and forth on straight needles:

Row 10 *P2 tog; rep from * to last 3 sts, ending p3 tog— 26 sts.

Row 11 *K2 tog; rep from *—13 sts.

Row 12 P1, *p2 tog; rep from *—7 sts.

For circular knitting:

Rnd 10 *K2 tog; rep from *—26 sts.

Rnd 11 *K2 tog; rep from *—13 sts.

Rnd 12 K1, *k2 tog; rep from *—7 sts

FINISHING

If knitting straight, sew back seam, reversing seam over first 4 in. from lower edge.

Weave in all ends. If using pom-pom, refer to instructions on p. 27.

FOLDING

To shape basic fold hat, fold bottom edge up 3 in.

For Robin Hood, fold same as basic fold hat, then fold brim in half again toward crown while pulling down at center front to form the point.

For rolled-brim hat, simply roll bottom edge to desired length.

For cloche, place basic fold hat on the back of your head and pull fold down at back of neck.

For miller's hat, just wear the hat without any folds, letting the top flop over.

Fanny

Using bulky novelty yarn, this hat can be created in just a few hours. You can also use a solid bulky yarn or a combination of yarns, but make sure that the gauge remains the same, and add your favorite flower.

SIZE

One size (fits average adult)

MATERIALS

Yarn

Skacel Fabio, 3½ oz./100 g skein; each about 88 yd./80 m:
• **A** Multi Blue/Purple 212–1 skein

Needles

• Size 10, or size required to obtain correct gauge

Other

- Tapestry needle
- ⅔ yd. purple grosgrain ribbon, 1⅜ in. wide
- Blue velvet rose

GAUGE

10 sts and 20 rows = 4 in. in garter st
To save time, take time to check gauge.

NOTES

Stitch counts in the directions include two garter selvage stitches for seaming.

The brim scallops are worked separately, then joined together to continue brim.

HAT

Brim

Make 9 scallops for brim edging as follows:
Cast on 5 sts.
Row 1 Knit.
Row 2 Cast on and k1 st, k5—6 sts.
Row 3 Cast on and k1 st, k6—7 sts.
Row 4 Cast on and k1 st, k7 —8 sts.
Row 5 Cast on and k1 st, k8—9 sts.
Cut yarn and push the finished scallop to the nonworking end of needle.
Make 8 more scallops in same way, casting on with a new strand of yarn for each scallop and pushing finished scallop to the nonworking end of needle with the others.
Do not cut yarn upon completing last scallop.

Next row Cast on 1 st for selvage; then knit across all 81 sts on needle to join scallops tog; cast on 1 st for selvage—83 sts [81 patt sts + 2 selvage sts].
Next 5 rows Knit.
Dec row K2, [k2 tog, k3; k2 tog, k2] 9 times—65 sts.
Next 3 rows Knit.
Dec row K2, [k2 tog, k5] 9 times—56 sts.
Place yarn marker for last dec row.
Work even in garter st until 6 in. from last dec row.

Crown

Row 1 K1, *k2 tog; rep from * to last st, k1—29 sts.
Row 2 Knit.
Row 3 K2, *k2 tog; rep from * to last st, k1—16 sts.
Row 4 Knit.
Row 5 K1, *k2 tog; rep from * to last st, k1—9 sts.
Row 6 K2, *k2 tog ; rep from * to last st, k1—6 sts.
Cut yarn, leaving long end. With tapestry needle, thread end through rem sts on needle.
Gather up and fasten securely.

FINISHING

Sew back seam.

Weave in all ends.

Pin ribbon band in place. Trim and seam to fit.

Referring to photo on facing page, turn brim back and sew in desired position. Attach rose.

Pillbox Hats

The pillbox hat has been a perennial fashion favorite ever since it was popularized by Jackie Kennedy. I've included five basic pillbox-shaped hats and used different techniques to shape and embellish each one.

Clockwise from top:
Flower Basket, Fringe Benefits,
Music Box

Music Box

This hat is knit from the top center down in one piece, using six different colors and a contrasting black. The musical notes are worked in duplicate stitch (upside down) after the hat has been knitted. The hat is lined with a knit 1, purl 1 ribbing for a nice fit and body shape.

SIZE

One size (fits average adult)

MATERIALS

Yarn

Rowan Designer Double Knitting, 1¾ oz./50 g skein; each about 126 yd./115 m:

- **mc** 1 skein each used in the following order:
- Tan 695
- Light Olive 664
- Mauve 694
- Light Yellow 623
- Lilac 628
- Salmon 689
- **cc** 1 skein:
- Black 062

Needles

- Size 5, or size required to obtain correct gauge

Other

- Tapestry needle
- Stitch markers

GAUGE

22 sts and 28 rows = 4 in. in st st
To save time, take time to check gauge.

NOTES

Stitch counts in the directions do not include two selvage stitches for seaming unless otherwise noted.

When changing colors, twist yarns on wrong side to prevent holes. Use separate balls of yarn for each of the six main color segments throughout. Over two-color charted areas, carry yarn not in use loosely across back of work. The musical note motif is not knit in but rather embroidered in duplicate stitch after hat is completed.

Hat is worked from center of crown to lower side edges.

HAT

Work in st st throughout unless otherwise noted.
With cc, cast on 10 sts [8 patt sts + 2 selvage sts].

Crown

Row 1 (rs) Inc in each st across—16 sts.
Row 2 Purl.
Row 3 Inc in every other st across—24 sts.
Row 4 Purl across, placing markers to divide work into 6 segments of 4 sts each.

Beg chart

Chart on facing page represents one of each of the 6 segments of the hat and begins with inc over row 5 as follows:
Inc row 5 *K2, inc in next st, k1; rep from * over each segment—30 sts [6 segments of 5 sts each—row 5 of chart completed].

Row 6 Purl with cc.

Cont chart, introduce mc for each segment worked in combination with cc as follows:

Row 7 *[K1, yo] with mc, k3 cc, [yo, k1] with mc; rep from *—42 sts [6 segments of 7 sts each].

Row 8 Work even.

Row 9 *[K1, yo, k2] with mc, k1 cc, [k2, yo, k1] with mc; rep from *—54 sts [6 segments of 9 sts each].

Row 10 Work even. Fasten off cc.

Rows 11-22 Cont over chart with mc only, inc 1 st at both sides of each color segment on rs rows by making a yo 1 st in from each side of every color segment—126 sts [6 segments of 21 sts each after row 21].

Turning ridge

Row 23 With cc, knit.

Row 24 With cc, knit dec 1 st over each segment—120 sts [20 sts each segment]. Fasten off cc.

Side sections

Rows 25-39 Cont to work even in st st with mc as established over each segment.

Rows 40-43 Reintroduce cc and work even over 2-color area of chart. Fasten off mc after row 43.

Cont with cc only as follows:

Row 44 Purl.

Turning ridge

Rows 45 & 46 Knit—chart ends after row 46. Fasten off cc.

Lining

With Tan, work in k1, p1 rib until lining measures same depth as body.

Bind off.

FINISHING

Sew back seams of hat and lining, gathering cast-on sts tog at center of crown.

Referring to photo on p. 56 and chart below and with cc, duplicate st musical note motif from chart in same direction as knitting over each segment.

Fold ribbed lining to inside of hat and sew in place to crown. Weave in all ends.

MUSIC BOX

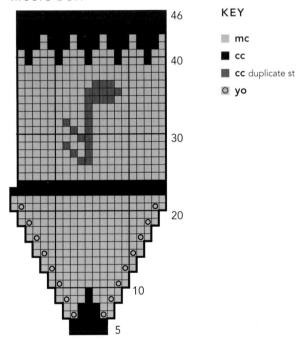

KEY

■ mc
■ cc
■ cc duplicate st
○ yo

Flower Basket

Begin this hat with the lining using stockinette stitch, and then work the body with a textured basket-weave stitch. The crown shaping is worked horizontally using short rows to achieve the round shape and is then sewn to the top of the hat. The flowers and the leaves are made and sewn on separately.

SIZE
One size (fits average adult)

MATERIALS

Yarn
Reynolds Paterna Handknitting Yarn, 1¾ oz./50 g skein; each about 110 yd./100 m:
- **A** Tan 135—2 skeins
- **B** Green 922—1 skein
- **C** Light Lilac 636—small amount
- **D** Lilac 616—small amount
- **E** Light Peach 994—small amount
- **F** Peach 830—small amount
- **G** Light Teal 745—small amount
- **H** Teal 725—small amount
- **J** Maize 431—small amount

Needles
- Sizes 5 and 7, or size required to obtain correct gauge

ther
Tapestry needle

GAUGE
20 sts and 28 rows = 4 in. in st st using larger needles
To save time, take time to check gauge.

NOTES
Stitch counts in the directions include two selvage stitches for seaming.

Hat is self-lined; instructions begin with lining.

When working crown, wrap yarn on short rows to prevent holes.

HAT
With larger needles and A, cast on 110 sts.
Work even in st st for 3¾ in. for lining; end ws.
Change to B.
K6 rows.
Change back to A and work basket-weave patt as follows:
Row 1 (rs) Knit.
Row 2 Purl.
Row 3 K2, *p4, k2; rep from * to end.
Row 4 P2, *k4, p2; rep from * to end.
Row 5 K2, *p4, k2; rep from * to end.
Row 6 P2, *k4, p2; rep from * to end.
Row 7 Knit.
Row 8 Purl.
Row 9 P3, *k2, p4; rep from * to last 5 sts, k2, p3.
Row 10 K3, *p2, k4; rep from * to last 5 sts, p2, k3.
Row 11 P3, *k2, p4; rep from * to last 5 sts, k2, p3.
Row 12 K3, *p2, k4; rep from * to last 5 sts, p2, k3.
Rep rows 1-12 once more.
Row 25 Knit.
Row 26 Purl.
Bind off.

Crown

With larger needles and A, cast on 17 sts.

Work short rows as follows: *K17, turn, p16, turn, k16, turn, p12, turn, k12, turn, p8, turn, k8, turn, p4, turn, k4, turn, p17, turn; rep from * 13 times more.

Bind off.

Flowers (make 3 of C and D, 2 of E and F, and 2 of G and H)

Flowers are worked from outer edge to center beg with dark color, changing to light color, and finishing with J for centers of all. Leave 8-in. end at color changes for seaming.

With smaller needles and dark color, cast on 58 sts.

Row 1 (ws) Knit.

Row 2 (rs) K3, *yo, k2, ssk, k2 tog, k2, yo, k1; rep from * to last st, end k1.

Row 3 Purl.

Row 4 K2, *yo, k2, ssk, k2 tog, k2, yo, k1; rep from * to last 2 sts, end k2.

Change to lighter color.

Row 5 Purl.

Row 6 *K1, k3 tog; rep from * to last 2 sts, end k2—30 sts.

Row 7 Purl.

Row 8 *K1, k3 tog; rep from * to last 2 sts, end k2—16 sts.

Change to J.

Row 9 Purl.

Row 10 K2 tog across—8 sts.

Cut yarn, leaving long end. With tapestry needle, thread end through rem sts on needle. Gather up and fasten securely.

Sew seam and weave in loose ends except for final tail of J, which will be used for sewing flowers to crown.

Leaves (make 14)

Leave a short tail when casting on and fastening off for attaching leaves to hat.

With smaller needles and B, cast on 5 sts.

Row 1 K2, yo, k1, yo, k2—7 sts.

Even rows 2-16 Purl.

Row 3 K3, yo, k1, yo, k3—9 sts.

Row 5 K4, yo, k1, yo, k4—11 sts.

Row 7 K5, yo, k1, yo, k5—13 sts.

Row 9 Ssk, k9, k2 tog—11 sts.

Row 11 Ssk, k7, k2 tog—9 sts.

Row 13 Ssk, k5, k2 tog—7 sts.

Row 15 Ssk, k3, k2 tog—5 sts.

Row 17 Ssk, k1, k2 tog—3 sts.

Row 18 P3 tog.

Fasten off.

FINISHING

Sew back seam of hat and lining.

Sew cast-on edge to bound-off edge of crown. Thread yarn through end stitches of every other row at center of crown; gather and fasten securely.

Sew crown in place.

Referring to photo on p. 56, attach flowers and leaves to top of hat.

Fold lining to inside of hat and sew in place to crown.

Fringe Benefits

I self-lined this hat with stockinette stitch and used a 10-spiral shaping for the crown. The hat is knit in one piece, and the fringe is knit separately and sewn on. It can be made without the fringe and folded for a lovely "go-anywhere" hat.

SIZE

One size (fits average adult)

MATERIALS

Yarn

Tahki Sable, 1¾ oz./50 g skein; each about 140 yd./128 m:
• **A** Blue 1634—2 skeins
Tahki Siena, 1¾ oz./50 g skein; each about 100 yd./92 m:
• **B** Blue Multicolor 8007—1 skein

Needles

• Size 5, or size required to obtain correct gauge

Other

• Stiffening material: 10-in. square buckram
• Tapestry needle

GAUGE

22 sts and 30 rows = 4 in. in st st
To save time, take time to check gauge.

NOTES

Stitch counts in the directions do not include two selvage stitches for seaming unless otherwise noted. Hat is self-lined; instructions begin with lining.

HAT

With A, cast on 112 sts [110 patt sts + 2 selvage sts]. Work even in st st for 10 in. for lining and outside of hat; end ws.

Turning ridge

P2 rows.

Crown

Row 1 *K2 tog, k9; rep from *—100 sts.
Even rows 2-18 Purl.
Row 3 *K2 tog, k8; rep from *—90 sts.
Row 5 *K2 tog, k7; rep from *—80 sts.
Row 7 *K2 tog, k6; rep from *—70 sts.
Row 9 *K2 tog, k5; rep from *—60 sts.
Row 11 *K2 tog, k4; rep from *—50 sts.
Row 13 *K2 tog, k3; rep from *—40 sts.
Row 15 *K2 tog, k2; rep from *—30 sts.
Row 17 *K2 tog, k1; rep from *—20 sts.
Row 19 *K2 tog; rep from *—10 sts.
Row 20 P2 tog—5 sts.
Cut yarn, leaving long end. With tapestry needle, thread end through rem sts on needle. Gather up and fasten securely.

Crown lining

With smaller needles and A, cast on 112 sts. Shape as for crown section.

FINISHING

Sew back seam of hat, crown, and lining.

FRINGE

With 2 strands of B, cast on 6 sts.

Work in garter st for 20 in.

Bind off 2 sts.

Sl rem sts off needle then *unravel 2 rows; knot gently near looped end; rep from * to end.

Referring to photo on p. 56, sew fringe around side of hat just under turning ridge.

Fold cast-on edge of lining to inside and sew to beg of crown.

Trace crown lining on buckram and cut just inside traced line. Position buckram between crown and crown lining; tack lining in place.

Weave in all ends.

Fold 1½ in. of doubled lower edge to rs for brim.

Black Cats

The cats on this hat are worked in intarsia using separate balls of color for the background and the cats. If you're superstitious about black cats, feel free to use any color for the cats or add a face with embroidery or beads, but stay away from squiggle eyes (no one likes a tacky cat). This hat begins with the lining and works from the bottom up.

SIZE

One size (fits average adult)

MATERIALS

Yarn

Plymouth Cleckheaton Country 8 Ply, 1¾ oz./50 g skein; each about 105 yd./96 m:
• **mc** Deep Orchid 1860–*or* Bright Yellow 1085–*or* Deep Pink 1856–2 skeins
• **cc** Black 006–1 skein *or* 1 ball of Black angora or chenille yarn of comparable weight as desired

Needles

• Sizes 4 and 5, or size required to obtain correct gauge

Other

• Tapestry needle
• Black cording: ⅜ in. to ½ in. in diameter, 21 in. long

GAUGE

22 sts and 30 rows = 4 in. in st st using larger needles
To save time, take time to check gauge.

NOTES

Stitch counts in the directions do not include two selvage stitches for seaming unless otherwise noted.

Read chart on p. 66 from right to left for right side rows and from left to right for wrong side rows.

Use separate balls of yarn for each color area. When changing colors, twist yarns on wrong side to prevent holes.

Hat is self-lined, instructions begin with lining.

HAT

With smaller needles and mc, cast on 116 sts [114 patt sts + 2 selvage sts].
Work in st st for 3¼ in. for lining; end rs.
Turning ridge (ws) Knit.
Change to larger needles.
Beg chart (rs) Cont in st st work 19-st rep of chart 6 times. When 25 rows of chart are completed, drop mc. Change to cc.
Next row (ws) Purl.
Following row (rs) Purl.
Cont in rev st st as established for 1 in.
Bind off ws.

Crown

With rs facing, fold rev st st band of cc down against rs of hat to expose color change. Leaving cc band unworked, with mc pick up and knit 112 sts [110 patt sts + 2 selvage sts] evenly from inside edge over mc sts of color change.
Next row and every alt row Purl.
Row 1 (rs) *Sl 1 knitwise, k2 tog, psso, k19; rep from *—100 sts.
Row 3 *Sl 1 knitwise, k2 tog, psso, k17; rep from *—90 sts.
Row 5 *Sl 1 knitwise, k2 tog, psso, k15; rep from *—80 sts.
Row 7 *Sl 1 knitwise, k2 tog, psso, k13; rep from *—70 sts.
Row 9 *Sl 1 knitwise, k2 tog, psso, k11; rep from *—60 sts.
Row 11 *Sl 1 knitwise, k2 tog, psso, k9; rep from *—50 sts.
Row 13 *Sl 1 knitwise, k2 tog, psso, k7; rep from *—40 sts.
Row 15 *Sl 1 knitwise, k2 tog, psso, k5; rep from *—30 sts.
Row 17 *Sl 1 knitwise, k2 tog, psso, k3; rep from *—20 sts.
Row 19 *Sl 1 knitwise, k2 tog, psso, k1; rep from *—10 sts.
Cut yarn, leaving long end. With tapestry needle, thread end through rem sts on needle. Gather up and fasten securely.

Clockwise from top:
Black Cats in angora, wool, chenille

BLACK CATS

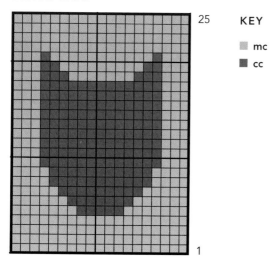

25

1

19-st repeat

KEY

▨ mc
■ cc

FINISHING

Sew back seam of hat.

Weave in all ends.

Fold lining to inside at turning row and stitch in place.

Sew short seam of cc band.

Place cording into natural roll of cc band, then carefully stitch long edge down around cording.

Jewel

The main body of this hat is worked horizontally with a six-row pattern stitch repeat. The crown is picked up at the top edge and worked in pattern stitch with decreases to shape the top. The lining is then picked up at the bottom edge and worked in knit 1, purl 1 ribbing. Floral tassels are crocheted in different lengths and sewn to the center top of the hat. If you use the suggested yarn, you'll have enough to make a second hat alternating the deep pink, periwinkle, and purple as A and the black as B, C, and D.

SIZE

One size (fits average adult)

MATERIALS

Yarn

Classic Elite Tapestry, 1¾ oz./50 g skein; each about 95 yd./87 m:

- **mc** 2 skeins:
- **A** Black 6713
- **cc** 1 skein each:
- **B** Deep Pink 6732
- **C** Periwinkle 6757
- **D** Purple 6759

Needles

- Size 5, or size required to obtain correct gauge
- Size F crochet hook

Other

- Tapestry needle

GAUGE

21 sts and 36 rows = 4 in. in knotted ridge patt
To save time, take time to check gauge.

NOTES

Stitch counts in the directions include two selvage stitches for seaming.

When changing colors for pattern stitch, carry main color (A) loosely up side of work; fasten off cc (B, C, and D) after finishing each ridge.

GLOSSARY

Knotted Ridge Pattern (multiple of 2 sts + 1)

Rows 1 & 3 (rs) With A, knit.

Rows 2 & 4 With A, purl.

Row 5 With B, k1, [k1, yo, k1] in next st, *sl 1 wyib, [k1, yo, k1] in next st; rep from * to last st, k1.

Row 6 With B, k1, k3 tog tbl, *sl 1 wyib, k3 tog tbl; rep from * to last st, k1.

Rows 7-10 Rep rows 1-4.

Rows 11 & 12 With C, rep rows 5 & 6.

Rows 13-16 Rep rows 1-4.

Rows 17 & 18 With D, rep rows 5 & 6.

Rep rows 1-18 for patt.

HAT

Body

With A, cast on 21 sts.
Rep rows 1-18 of knotted ridge patt 10 times; then work rows 1 and 2 once—182 rows.
Bind off.

Crown

With rs facing and A, pick up and k123 sts evenly across one long edge of side piece.

Next row (ws) Knit.

Beg patt

Row 1 (rs) With A, knit.

Row 2 With A, purl.

Row 3 With A, k1, *sl 1, k2 tog, psso, k8; rep from * to last st, k1—101 sts.

Row 4 With A, purl.

Row 5 With B, k1, [k1, yo, k1] in next st, *sl 1 wyib, [k1, yo, k1] in next st; rep from * to last st, k1.

Row 6 With B, k1, k3 tog tbl, *sl 1 wyib, k3 tog tbl; rep from * to last st, k1.

Rows 7 & 8 Rep rows 1 & 2.

Row 9 With A, k1, *sl 1, k2 tog, psso, k6; rep from * to last st, k1—79 sts.

Row 10 With A, purl.

Rows 11 & 12 With C, rep rows 5 & 6.

Rows 13 & 14 Rep rows 1 & 2.

Row 15 With A, k1, *sl 1, k2 tog, psso, k4; rep from * to last st, k1—57 sts.

Row 16 With A, purl.

Rows 17 & 18 With D, rep rows 5 & 6.

Rows 19 & 20 Rep rows 1 & 2.

Row 21 With A, k1, *sl 1, k2 tog, psso, k2; rep from * to last st, k1—35 sts.

Row 22 With A, purl.

Rows 23 & 24 With B, rep rows 5 & 6.

Row 25 With A, k1, *k2 tog; rep from *—18 sts.

Row 26 With A, purl.

Row 27 With A, k2 tog across—9 sts.

Row 28 With A, p1, *p2 tog; rep from *—5 sts.

Cut yarn, leaving long end. With tapestry needle, thread end through rem sts on needle. Gather up and fasten securely.

Lining

With rs of bottom edge facing and A, pick up and k94 sts evenly across.

Next row (ws) Knit.

Cont with A, work in k1, p1 rib for 1 in.; end ws.

Change to D, k 1 row.

Cont with D, resume k1, p1 rib for 1 in.; end ws.

Change to B, k 1 row.

Cont with B, resume k1, p1 rib, and work even until lining depth matches side.

Bind off.

FINISHING

Weave in all ends.

Sew cast-on edge of body to bound-off edge of body.

Sew crown lining seam. Fold lining to inside and sew to beg of crown.

CROCHETED FLORAL TASSELS
(make 1 each of B, C, and D)

With crochet hook and double strand of yarn, ch 32 with B, 40 with C, and 46 with D.

Sl st in the 7th ch from hook, [ch 7, sl st in same ch as before] 4 times.

Fasten off and weave in final end.

Sew beg of each tassel to center of crown. Referring to photo on facing page, tack tassel in desired position at side of crown.

Anything Goes

The hats in this chapter are my personal favorites. You'll find a two-sided snowflake with a straight top seam, a helmet-shaped hat that folds into a brim hat, a traditional hunting-style hat, a cable knit with a ball top, and a square-top hat with two-color instarsia. All of these hats are geared toward cold weather. They warm the head as well as the heart.

Clockwise from top:
Elmer, Double-Take Snowflake, Pom-Pom-Pom

Double-Take Snowflake

This hat can be worn at any angle to give you several different looks. One light color and one dark color work best on the contrasting snowflake. If you prefer a more traditional top shaping, refer to Chapter 1 for a simple knit 2 together decrease shaping.

SIZE

One size (fits average adult)

MATERIALS

Yarn

Reynolds Lite-Lopi, 1¾ oz./50 g skein; each about 109 yd./100 m:
- **A** Dark Gray Heather 5—1 skein
- **B** Light Gray Heather 54—1 skein

Needles

- Sizes 4 and 6, or size required to obtain correct gauge
- Size G crochet hook

Other

- Tapestry needle
- Cardboard for tassel: 4 in. long

GAUGE

18 sts and 24 rows = 4 in. in st st using larger needles
To save time, take time to check gauge.

NOTES

Stitch counts in the directions include two selvage stitches for seaming.

Read chart on facing page from right to left for right side rows and from left to right for wrong side rows.

Use separate balls of yarn for each major color area. When changing colors, twist yarns on wrong side to prevent holes. Carry yarn not in use loosely across snowflakes on wrong side of work.

HAT

With smaller needles and A, cast on 110 sts [108 patt sts + 2 selvage sts].
Row 1 (rs) *K2, p2; rep from *, end k2.
Row 2 *P2, k2; rep from *, end p2.
Rep rows 1 and 2 for rib until 3½ in. from beg; end rs.
Change to larger needles and st st.
Next row (ws) Purl across, inc 2 sts evenly—112 sts [110 patt sts + 2 selvage sts].
Beg chart
Chart includes selvage sts for seaming.
Beg on rs with row 1, work chart through row 37.
Next row: Bind off.

FINISHING

Sew side seam, reversing seam over first half of rib for brim.

With ws tog, fold hat flat with seam at one side and inside fold line as indicated on chart at other side.

Pleat each top side edge as follows: Tuck inside fold/seam lines to inside of hat until outside fold lines meet. Pin, then baste in place.

With rs facing, crochet hook, and A, chain through all thicknesses across top to join.

TASSELS *(make 1 of A and 1 of B)*

Wrap yarn 40 times around 4-in. length of cardboard.

Thread long strand of yarn under wraps at one end and knot.

Cut yarn at opposite end along edge of cardboard.

Wrap the tassel tightly with 1 strand of cc yarn about 1 in. from tied end, then thread yarn back through top of tassel.

Trim evenly. Attach tassels to each side of top as shown in photo on p. 70.

DOUBLE-TAKE SNOWFLAKE

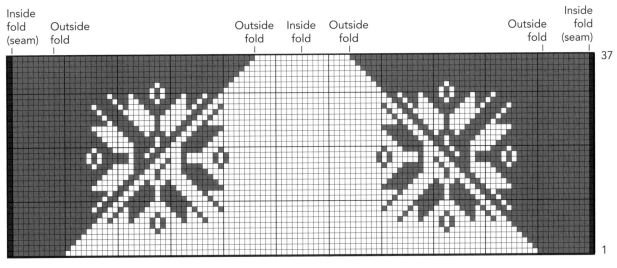

112 sts

KEY

■ Selvage st

▨ A

☐ B

Pom-Pom-Pom

As a child I had a version of this hat knitted by an aunt. I loved the way I could wear it up or down and still do. If you don't use the Oggi yarn, use a comparably soft yarn, as the hat will come in contact with your face and neck.

SIZE
One size (fits average adult)

MATERIALS

Yarn
Stacy Charles Filitura di Crosa Alpaca Oggi, 1¾ oz./50 g skein; each about 82 yd./75 m:
- **A** Forest Green 224—3 skeins
- **B** Red 17—1 skein
- **C** Gray 204—1 skein

Needles
- Size 8, or size required to obtain correct gauge

Other
- Tapestry needle
- Cardboard for pom-poms

GAUGE
26 sts and 24 rows = 4 in. in unstretched k2, p2 rib
To save time, take time to check gauge.

NOTES
Stitch counts in the directions include two selvage stitches for seaming.

Each color change begins with right side row. Knit the first row of each color change then resume rib pattern on following rows.

HAT
With A, cast on 110 sts.
Row 1 (rs) *K2, p2; rep from *, end k2.
Row 2 *P2, k2; rep from *, end p2.
Rep rows 1 and 2 for rib pat.
Work even in rib until 7½ in. from beg; end rs.

Face opening
Maintain rib patt as established.
Row 1 (ws) Work first 34 sts; bind off center 42 sts in patt; work rem 34 sts.
Next row (rs) Work first 34 sts; cast on 42 sts over the bound-off sts of face opening; work rem 34 sts.
Cont in rib as established over all sts until 9 in. from beg; end ws.
Fasten off A.

Stripes
Change to B.
Row 1 (rs) Knit.
Rows 2 -10 Resume rib patt as previously established.
Change to A.
Rows 11-20 Rep rows 1-10.

Change to C.

Rows 21-30 Rep rows 1-10.

Change to A.

Next row (rs) Knit.

Next row (ws) Work in rib as established.

Top shaping

Row 1 (rs) *K2 tog, p2 tog; rep from *—55 sts.

Row 2 P2 tog across to last st, p1—28 sts.

Row 3 K2 tog across—14 sts.

Row 4 P2 tog across—7 sts.

Cut yarn, leaving long end. With tapestry needle, thread yarn through rem sts on needle. Gather up and fasten securely.

FINISHING

Sew back seam of hat.

Weave in all ends.

CORKSCREW TASSELS
(make 3, one of each cast-on length)

With A, cast on 20, 30, and 40 sts.

Row 1 Knit into front, then back, then front of each st before slipping it from needle.

Row 2 Bind off in purl.

Attach one end of each tassel to center top of hat.

Twist each tassel to form corkscrew.

POM-POMS *(make one each of A, B, and C)*

Cut two 4¼-in. cardboard circles. Cut ¾-in. hole in center of each.

Cut small wedge of each donut shape away to make it easier to wrap yarn.

Place circles tog and wrap yarn 150 times around donut shape.

Insert scissors between cardboard and carefully cut around outer edge to release yarn.

Slip a length of yarn between cardboard circles and knot tightly. Gently ease cardboard from the pom-pom. Trim to neaten shape.

Referring to photo at left, attach 1 pom-pom to the end of each corkscrew tassel.

Elmer

As in Fudd! This hat works just as well without the plaid motif, but make your solid colors with contrasting fur to maintain the fun spirit of the hat. The structure of the hat allows you to wear it with the flaps up or down to cover the ears.

SIZE
One size (fits average adult)

MATERIALS

Yarn
Lane Borgosesia Knitaly, 3½ oz./100 g skein; each about 215 yd./196 m:
- **A** Red 3793–2 skeins
- **B** Black Nero–2 skeins

Skacel Merino Fur, 1¾ oz./50 g skein; each about 44 yd./40 m:
- **C** Black 65–2 skeins

Needles
- Sizes 5 and 6, or size required to obtain correct gauge
- Size 3 double-pointed needles

Other
- Tapestry needle
- Bobbins

GAUGE
18 sts and 24 rows = 4 in. in st st using double strand of Knitaly and larger needles
15 sts and 30 rows = 4 in. in garter st using 1 strand of C and larger needles
To save time, take time to check gauge.

NOTES
Stitch counts in the directions include two selvage stitches for seaming.

Hat is worked in blocks with 2 strands of A, 2 strands of B, or 1 strand each of A and B held together as indicated in charts on p. 81.

Ear flap and visor linings are worked with 1 strand of C.

Read charts from right to left for right side rows and from left to right for wrong side rows.

Cut one 4½-yd. length of A and wind onto 1 small bobbin.

Cut five 10-yd. lengths of A and wind onto 5 bobbins.

Cut six 10-yd. lengths of B and wind onto 6 bobbins.

Use one ball of A for rows 1-10 of chart 1, adding separate second-color bobbin for each color block according to chart. When changing colors, twist yarns on wrong side to prevent holes.

Use one ball of B for rows 11-20 of chart 1, adding separate second-color bobbin for each color block according to chart. When changing colors, twist yarns on wrong side to prevent holes.

GLOSSARY

I-Cord

With double-pointed needles, cast on 3 sts. *Knit across. Do not turn work. Push the sts back to rh end of needle. Pull to tighten and rep from * until cord measures desired length. Bind off.

HAT

With smaller needles and a single strand of B, cast on 108 sts.

Work in k1, p1 rib for 1¼ in.

Turning ridge (ws) Knit across dec 10 sts evenly—98 sts [96 patt sts + 2 selvage sts].

Beg chart 1

Change to larger needles and st st using 2 strands of yarn held tog.

Keep selvage sts in st st and rep 20 rows of chart for patt.

Row 1 (rs) Work 16-st rep of chart 6 times.

Cont to work from chart as established for 4 in.

Crown

Row 1 (rs) [K3, k2 tog, k3] over 8 sts of each color block across—86 sts.

Row 2 Work even—each block has 7 sts.

Row 3 [K1, k2 tog, k1, k2 tog, k1] over 7 sts of each color block across—62 sts.

Rows 4-8 Work even—each block has 5 sts.

Row 9 [K2 tog, k1, k2 tog] over 5 sts of each color block across—38 sts.

Row 10 Work even—each block has 3 sts.

Row 11 [K2 tog, k1] over 3 sts of each color block across—26 sts.

Row 12 P2 tog over 2 sts of each color block across—14 sts.

Row 13 K1, [k2 tog] 6 times, k1—8 sts.

Cut yarn, leaving long end. With tapestry needle, thread end through rem sts on needle. Gather up and fasten securely.

EAR FLAPS

Sew back seam. Fold ribbing to inside along turning ridge and stitch in place. With inside still facing, count over 4 color blocks to right of back seam.

With larger needles and 2 strands of B, pick up 64 sts along turning ridge, ending 4 color blocks to left of back seam. Turn so rs is facing.

Beg chart 2

Work in st st with 2 strands of yarn held tog as indicated and rep 20 rows of chart for patt as follows:

Row 1 (rs) Work 16-st rep of chart 4 times.

Cont chart through row 10.

Row 11 (rs) Work 16 sts for first ear flap; join 2 strands of B, bind off next 32 sts to complete back; work rem 16 sts in patt for other ear flap.

Work both flaps at same time with separate balls of yarn, and cont chart as established over each flap as follows:

Row 12 (ws) Purl.

Row 13 Dec 1 st at back (inside) edge of each flap.

Rows 14 & 15 Rep last 2 rows once—14 sts each ear flap.

Rows 16-20 Work even over 14 sts of each flap.

Row 21 Dec 1 st at both edges of each ear flap—12 sts.
Row 22 Purl.
Rows 23-29 Rep last 2 rows until 4 sts rem each flap; end rs.
Row 30 Bind off purlwise.

Fur lining

With larger needles and 1 strand of C, cast on 55 sts.
Work in garter st until 2 in. from beg.
Next row K14 for first ear flap; join a second ball of yarn and bind off center 27 sts to complete back, k14 for rem ear flap.
Cont in garter st throughout, work both flaps at the same time with separate balls of yarn as follows:
Next row Knit.
Following row Dec 1 st at back (inside) edge of each flap.
Rep last 2 rows once—12 sts each ear flap.
Work even over 12 sts of each flap for 4 more rows.
Next row Dec one st at both edges of each ear flap.
Following row Knit.
Rep last 2 rows until 4 sts rem each flap.
Bind off.

VISOR

With ws facing, larger needles, and 2 strands of B, pick up rem 32 sts across front of hat. Turn, rs facing.
Beg chart 2
Work in st st with 2 strands of yarn held tog as indicated throughout.
Row 1 (rs) Work 16-st rep of chart twice.
Cont chart until 1½ in. from beg; end ws.
Dec 1 st each end of next row.
P1 row.
Then, dec 1 st each end of every row until 18 sts rem.
Bind off.

Fur lining

With larger needles and 1 strand of C, cast on 26 sts.
Work in garter st until 1½ in. from beg.
Cont in garter st throughout.
Next row Dec 1 st at each end.
Next row Knit.
Then dec 1 st at each end of every row until 12 sts rem.
Bind off.

FINISHING

With ws tog, pin fur linings to ear flaps and visor.
From plaid side with B, sew outside edges of hat to fur linings with blanket st.
Sew inside edges of fur lining to base of turning ridge.
Weave in all ends.

TIES

With double-pointed needles and a single strand of B, work two 15½-in. lengths of I-cord. Referring to photo on p. 78, sew one end of each cord to bottom of each ear flap; knot rem end.

BLANKET STITCH

Bring thread out on lower edge and insert needle in position on upper edge, taking straight downward stitch with thread under needle point. Pull up stitch to form loop; repeat.

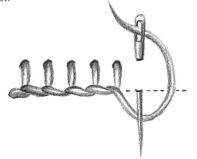

ELMER

Chart 1

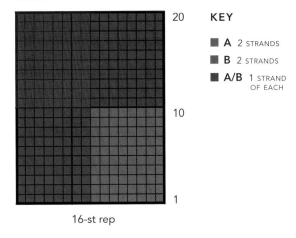

16-st rep

Chart 2

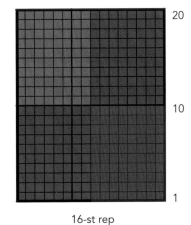

16-st rep

KEY

■ **A** 2 STRANDS
■ **B** 2 STRANDS
■ **A/B** 1 STRAND OF EACH

Roman Cable

I designed the cables to converge and meet at the top of this hat. A Styrofoam ball supports the cabled pom-pom. The hat is made with an easy-care acrylic fiber, but remember to remove the ball before you wash and dry it to maintain its shape, or use polyester fiberfill in place of the ball.

SIZE

One size (fits average adult)

MATERIALS

Yarn

Bernat Berella "4", Monsanto Bounce Back Fibers, 3½ oz./100 g skein; each about 240 yd./220 m:
• Geranium 8929–1 skein

Needles

• Sizes 5 and 7, or size required to obtain correct gauge
• Cable needle

Other

• Tapestry needle
• One 2-in. Styrofoam ball or polyester fiberfill (small amount)

GAUGE

20 sts and 28 rows = 4 in. in st st using larger needles
To save time, take time to check gauge.

NOTES

Stitch counts in the directions include two selvage stitches for seaming.

Gauge is given over st st. Correct st st gauge will result in proper fit over cable pat.

GLOSSARY

C4F Sl 2 sts to cn and hold at front of work, k2, k2 from cn.

HAT

With smaller needles, cast on 122 sts [120 patt sts + 2 selvage sts].
Work in k1, p1 rib for 4 rows; end rs.
Change to larger needles and establish cable placement as follows:
Setup row (ws) K4, *p4, k6; rep from * across, end last rep k4.
Row 1 (rs) P4, *C4F, p6; rep from * across, end last rep p4.

Row 2 (ws) K4, *p4, k6; rep from * across, end last rep k4.
Cont over established cable placement as follows:
Rows 3, 5, 9 & 11 (rs) P4, *k4, p6; rep from * across, end last rep p4.
Rows 4, 6, 8, 10 & 12 (ws) Knit the knit sts and purl the purl sts as they face you.
Row 7 P4, *C4F, p6; rep from * across, end last rep p4.
Dec row 13 P2, *p2 tog, C4F, p2 tog, p2; rep from * across—98 sts.
Row 14 K3, *p4, k4; rep from * across, end last rep k3.
Cont over newly established cable placement as follows:
Rows 1, 3, 7 & 9 (rs) P3, *k4, p4; rep from * across, end last rep p3.
Rows 2, 4, 6, 8 & 10 (ws) Knit the knit sts and purl the purl sts as they face you.
Row 5 P3, *C4F, p4; rep from * across, end last rep p3.
Dec row 11 P1, p2 tog, *C4F, [p2 tog] twice; rep from * across, end last rep p2 tog once, p1—74 sts.
Row 12 K2, *p4, k2; rep from *.
Cont over newly established cable placement as follows:
Rows 1, 3, 7, & 9 (rs) P2, *k4, p2; rep from *.
Rows 2, 4, 6, 8 & 10 (ws) Knit the knit sts and purl the purl sts as they face you.
Row 5 (rs/cable) P2, *C4F, p2; rep from *.
Row 11 (rs/cable/dec) P2, *C4F, p2 tog; rep from *— 62 sts.
Row 12 [K1, p4] across to last 2 sts, k2.
Cont over newly established cable placement as follows:
Rows 1 & 3 (rs) P2, *k4, p1; rep from *.
Rows 2 & 4 (ws) [K1, p4] across to last 2 sts, k2.
Row 5 (rs/cable) P2, *C4F, p1; rep from *. MARK ROW.
Row 6 (ws/dec) [K1, p4 tog, k1, p4] across to last 2 sts, k2—44 sts

BALL

Row 1 (rs/dec) P2, *k4, p3 tog; rep from *—32 sts.
Rows 2, 4, 6, 8 & 10 [K1, p4] across to last 2 sts, k2.
Rows 3, 7 & 9 P2, *k4, p1; rep from *.
Row 5 & 11 (rs/cable) P2, *C4F, p1; rep from *.
Row 12 (ws/dec) [K1, p4 tog] across to last 2 sts, k2—14 sts.
Row 13 (rs/dec) K2 tog across—7 sts.
Row 14 Purl.
Cut yarn, leaving long end. With tapestry needle, thread end through rem sts on needle. Gather up and fasten securely.

FINISHING

Sew back seam of hat.

Insert Styrofoam ball or polyester fiberfill.

With tapestry needle, weave length of yarn behind each cable twist of marked row just under ball; fasten securely to inside and tie. When washing, untie and remove ball; reinsert after washing and regather.

Weave in all ends.

Fleur-de-Lys

I've incorporated the royal French fleur-de-lys symbol on-to a peasant-style hat. The hat is knit from the bottom up in stockinette stitch, which forms a rolled edge. The motif is worked in intarsia as the hat is knit. The square top is knitted separately and crocheted from the right side to the top of the hat to complete the shape. Cross-stitches are then worked around the seam for the rustic peasant ef-fect, and the tassels are sewn to three corners of the crown. Viva le France!

SIZE

One size (fits average adult)

MATERIALS

Yarn

Reynolds Lopi, 3½ oz./100 g skein; each about 110 yd./100 m:
- **A** Teal 0101—2 skeins
- **B** Gold 0332—1 skein

Needles

- Sizes 8 and 10, or size required to obtain correct gauge
- Size J crochet hook

Other

- Tapestry needle
- Cardboard: 4½ in. by 3 in.

GAUGE

14 sts and 20 rows = 4 in. in st st using larger needles
To save time, take time to check gauge.

NOTES

Stitch counts in the directions include two selvage stitches for seaming.

Read chart from right to left for right side rows and from left to right for wrong side rows.

Use separate balls of yarn for each color area. When changing colors, twist yarns on wrong side to prevent holes.

HAT

With smaller needles and A, cast on 77 sts [75 patt sts + 2 selvage sts].
Work in st st for 2½ in.
Change to larger needles and work even until 3 in. from beg; end ws.
Beg chart (rs) Work selvage st, then work 25-st chart rep 3 times, work selvage st. When 22 rows of chart are completed, cont with A until 9¼ in. from beg.
Bind off.

Crown

With larger needles and A, cast on 19 sts.
Work in st st for 27 rows.
Crown measures approximately 5½ in. square.
Bind off.

FINISHING

Sew back seam, reversing first 2½ in. for bottom roll.

Pin edges of crown to top edge, distributing fabric evenly around and aligning back seam and corner of crown.

With rs facing, crochet hook, and A, chain through both thicknesses around to join.

With B, work cross sts around crown over crocheted join.

Weave in all ends.

TASSELS *(make 3 of B)*

Wrap yarn 40 times around 4½-in. length of cardboard.

Thread long strand of yarn under wraps at one end and knot.

Cut yarn at opposite end along edge of cardboard.

Wrap tassel tightly with 1 strand of yarn about 1 in. from tied end, then thread yarn back through top of tassel. Trim evenly.

Referring to photo on facing page, attach tassels to 3 corners of the crown.

CROSS-STITCH

Bring needle through on lower right line of cross, and insert at top left of same line, taking stitch through fabric to lower left line (A). Continue to end of row in this way; on return, complete other half of cross (B). Top strands of all stitches should point in same direction.

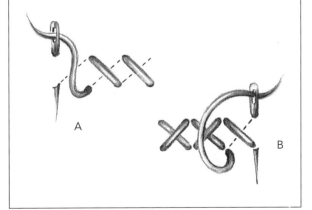

A   B

FLEUR-de-LYS

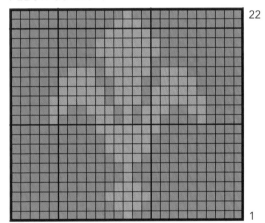

22

1

25-st repeat

KEY

■ A

■ B

Resources

Yarns Used

Bernat
(distributed by Spinrite Yarns)
P.O. Box 40
Listowel, Ont., N4W 3H3
Canada

Classic Elite
12 Perkins St.
Lowell, MA 01854

Crystal Palace
3006 San Pablo Ave.
Berkeley, CA 94702

Estelle Designs and Sales Ltd.
Units 65/67
2220 Midland Ave.
Scarborough, Ont., M1P 3E6
Canada

Lane Borgosesia
P.O. Box 217
Colorado Springs, CO 80903

Lion Brand
34 West 15th St.
New York, NY 10011
800-258-9276
Sells retail as well as wholesale

Plymouth Yarn Co.
P.O. Box 28
Bristol, PA 19007

Reynolds
(distributed by JCA, Inc.)
35 Scales Ln.
Townsend, MA 01469

Rowan
(distributed by Westminster Fibers in U. S.)
(distributed by Estelle Designs and Sales Ltd. in Canada)
5 Northern Blvd.
Amherst, NH 03031

Skacel
11612 S.E. 196th St.
Renton, WA 98058
(253) 854-2710 (call for store nearest you)

Stacy Charles
1061 Manhattan Ave.
Brooklyn, NY 11222

Stahl Wolle
(distributed by Tahki in U. S.)
(distributed by Diamond Yarn in Canada)
9697 St. Laurent
Montreal, Que., H3L 2N1
Canada

Tahki
11 Graphic Pl.
Moonachie, NJ 07074

Mail Order Sources

Abbey Yarns and Kits
1512 Myers Rd.
Marion, OH 43302
(800) 999-5648, (614) 389-1461
Classic Elite, Crystal Palace, Lane Borgosesia, Plymouth, Reynolds, Rowan, Skacel, Stacy Charles, Tahki

C.A.T.S. Group
4-A Brocket Rd.
Welwyn Garden City
AL8 7TY England
(01707) 268471

Earthsong Fibers
5115 Excelsior Blvd. #428
Minneapolis, MN 55416
(800) 473-5350, (612) 926-1201
Crystal Palace, Stahl Wolle, Tahki

Ernel Yarns
1419 Burlingame Ave. #G
Burlingame, CA 94010
(800) 343-4874, (415) 344-5050
Classic Elite, Reynolds, Stacy Charles

Great Yarns
1208 Ridge Rd.
Raleigh, NC 27607
(800) 810-0045, (919) 832-3599
Classic Elite, Lane Borgosesia, Reynolds, Skacel, Stacy
Charles, Tahki

Imagiknit 2000
3493 Bayou Rd., RR #3
Orillia, Ont., L3V 6H3
Canada
(800) 318-9426
Reynolds, Rowan

Martha Hall Natural Fiber Yarns
20 Bartol Island Rd.
Freeport, ME 04032
(800) 643-4566
Classic Elite, Crystal Palace, Lane Borgosesia, Plymouth,
Reynolds, Tahki

Patternworks
36A South Gate Dr.
Poughkeepsie, NY 12601
(800) 438-5464, (914) 462-8000
Classic Elite, Crystal Palace, Lane Borgosesia, Plymouth,
Reynolds, Skacel, Stahl Wolle, Tahki

Personal Threads
8025 West Dodge Rd.
Omaha, NE 68114
(800) 306-7733, (402) 391-7733
Classic Elite, Crystal Palace, Lane Borgosesia, Plymouth,
Reynolds, Rowan, Skacel, Stacy Charles, Tahki

Ram Wools
143 Smith St.
Winnipeg, Man., R3C 1J5
Canada
(800) 263-8002
Classic Elite, Rowan

Webs Yarn Merchants
P.O. Box 147
Northampton, MA 01061
(413) 584-2225
Classic Elite, Lane Borgosesia, Plymouth, Reynolds,
Skacel, Stahl Wolle, Tahki

The Wool Connection
34 East Main St.,
Old Avon Village N.
Avon, CT 06001
(800) 933-9665, (860) 678-1710
Classic Elite, Crystal Palace, Lane Borgosesia, Plymouth,
Stacy Charles, Stahl Wolle, Tahki

Woolgathering
750 Calico Ct.
Waukesha, WI 53186
(888) 248-3225, (414) 798-1466
Classic Elite, Lane Borgosesia, Reynolds, Rowan, Skacel,
Stacy Charles, Stahl Wolle, Tahki

Yarn Express
120 Moultonville Rd.
Center Ossipee, NH 03814
(800) 432-1886, (603) 539-4397
Bernat, Classic Elite, Crystal Palace, Lane Borgosesia,
Plymouth, Reynolds, Rowan, Skacel, Stacy Charles, Stahl
Wolle, Tahki

BOOK PUBLISHER: Jim Childs
ACQUISITIONS EDITOR: Jolynn Gower
PUBLISHING COORDINATOR: Sarah Coe

KNITTING EDITOR: Sonja Dagress
TECHNICAL CONSULTANT: Dorothy Ratigan

EDITOR: Carolyn Mandarano
DESIGNER/LAYOUT ARTIST: Carol Singer
ILLUSTRATOR: Rosalie Vaccaro
PHOTOGRAPHERS: Marcus Tullis (except where noted);
Scott Phillips (p. ii, v, vi, 78)

TYPEFACE: Berkeley Old Style, Avenir
PAPER: 70-lb. Patina
PRINTER: Quebecor Printing/Kingsport, Kingsport, Tennessee